LIVING
THE
GUIDED
LIFE

A Path to
CONSCIOUS CONNECTION
with your Inner Guide

CHRIS LAURETIG

For Jane, Abigail and Charlie

CONTENTS

Part 1
UNDERSTANDING YOUR INNER GUIDE

_____ Chapter 1 _____
INNER GUIDANCE

It was Monday morning and as usual, I was sitting at my desk, anticipating what difficulty would walk through my door in the form of my students. You see, I am the vocational teacher and intervention specialist at an alternative high school, Alpha Tech, for students with emotional and behavioral difficulties. Each day my students bring with them their stories and difficulties with life.

Before I move on with the rest of my story of this early spring day in Cleveland, Ohio, it is important to clarify a few things. My students are no different than you and I, we all have emotional and behavioral struggles. In the eyes of our society these teenagers' emotional and behavioral struggles have risen to the level of requiring a significant intervention, namely being placed in an alternative school with staff members who are trained to help them. But the core issues that brought the students to Alpha Tech are the same as the core issues that cause you and I to overeat, not exercise, be unhappy in our work or relationships, limit our connection with our Inner Guidance and so on.

Now back to the story. One of the last students to arrive on this particular day was Brad. A wonderful 16 year old who was engaging, intelligent, hard working, handsome, funny and A COMPLETE MESS. By complete mess, I mean that he was miserable 95% of the time. He hated coming to school, he hated being at home, he even hated going to sleep and he seemed unable to complete or follow through on almost any task.

On this particular day Brad was scheduled to go to his vocational experience first thing in the morning. My students split their days, half vocational and half academic. Brad stormed into my office, flopped down on the couch and announced, "There is no fucking way I am going to vocational this morning." At this point he went on a several minute rant about how miserable he was feeling and because of this he would be unable to function.

I realized that I needed to put on my coaching hat and see if I could help Brad turn things around so that he could function. Although my job duties are primarily vocational in nature, after years of working with this student population I have learned to coach them through many upsets.

I went through the usual questioning. "Why are you so upset?" "Is there something in particular that has you so upset that you can't function?" "Did something specifically bad happen last night or this morning that is upsetting you." All to no avail, Brad was unable to identify any issue or thought that was causing him to shut down. He just knew he felt like crap and did not want to deal with any one or have to do anything.

This was not an unusual state for Brad. Despite his capabilities he often found himself feeling miserable to the point of being unable to function.

After about ten minutes of questioning he became even more agitated. He was essentially saying to me, "Just leave me alone, ask nothing of me and give me permission to go home." I decided to shut up, as my "Coaching" was getting nowhere. I sat back in silence and just let Brad writhe on the couch for a few moments.

Over the years I had become quite proud of my ability to help my students shift their perspective and work through their upsets. I thought myself quite clever and prided myself on students leaving my office with some greater sense of well-being then when they entered. More recently though I had begun to experiment with the idea that maybe, just maybe, I was not the ultimate source of information for helping my students. That possibly there was a source of information beyond my rational mind that could offer help that I might not be readily aware of.

There are always those moments where no matter what I say or no matter what technique I use, my student is unable to make a shift. It was in these moments that I began my experiment.

I had been learning for years that I had an Inner Guide that was always available and had answers to life's struggles that lead to peace. The question for me was always, "How do I access this wisdom." It turns out, I only need to ask and the assistance that is always available comes into my awareness. The rest of this book is about how to prepare your mind to easily access your Inner Guide.

In this silent moment in my office with Brad, I asked for help. I had reached a point where I had exhausted my personal toolbox of techniques and did not know what to do. I came to find out that Acknowledging that, **"I don't know"** was a very important step in accepting guidance. I will explain more about "Not Knowing" later.

I received very clear guidance on that beautiful spring morning in Cleveland. I was to show Brad the "Responsibility Ladder."

Naturally, your next question is, "What is The Responsibility Ladder? Is it some sort of medieval torture device used to punish those who don't take responsibility for their lives?" No, nothing quite that exciting. It is actually a concept developed by my dear friend Bruce Schaffer that uses the graphic of a ladder to help people understand that they choose to take different levels of responsibility for their lives. Brad had been through several trainings on the Responsibility Ladder concepts.

In the moment and using what we might call my rational mind or intellect, this made no sense. The concepts that are dealt with in the responsibility ladder seemed to be irrelevant and even off topic. But, the guidance was so clear that I set aside my "Rational" concerns about this method of intervention and reached into my desk drawer for the written example of the Ladder. I thought, "Maybe the Ladder will spark some sort of a conversation that will get to the core of what's bothering Brad and he can move on."

I rolled my high back leather office chair over to the couch where Brad lay in complete consternation and emotional pain, with the "Ladder" in my hand. The exchange went as follows:

"I want to show you something."

Brad replied with complete disdain and disgust, "What?"

"The Responsibility Ladder."

"What the fuck, I've seen that shit before."

"I know, but I think it might help."

"Fuck that, I don't want to look at anything and that stuff is bullshit anyway."

"I know, but just let me go over it with you."

With a sigh of resignation Brad passively allowed me to review the concepts in the Responsibility Ladder with him. There are five rungs and the wording for each rung is only a few sentences long. This review took only about a minute.

Once finished, I eased my chair back from the couch in anticipation of what this review might spark. Before I was even done pushing away from the couch Brad sat up. His facial expression had shifted and he looked at ease. He announced that he was ready to go to "Vocational."

I said, "What?" in total surprise.

Standing up he replied, "I am ready to go to Vocational now."

I asked, "Why?"

He stretched and said, "I don't know, I feel fine now."

"What happened, why do you feel fine?" I asked. Now it was my turn to be in consternation.

"I don't know."

"Was there something in the Responsibility Ladder that helped you make sense of your upset?"

"No, not really, not that I can think of"

"What is it about what just happened that helped you feel better?" My intellect was begging for an explanation for this miraculous turnaround.

"I really have no idea, I feel just fine and am ready to go."

I sat there dumbfounded as Brad headed out the door like a new person. Although I had asked for and received guidance before, it always seemed to lead to some type of rational exchange between my student and me. This was new territory for me.

I did not need to understand anything? This was certainly turning my coaching world upside down. I did not need to figure out what was bothering Brad to help him understand it in a more peaceful or productive way. I had been taught that my Inner Guide has access to and can make use of information that I am not aware of, and therefore come up with answers that my intellect could not.

In previous experiences of receiving guidance I was aware of the answers not being obvious to me before I asked for help. But in the past these guided moments made sense. I could say to myself, "Oh yeah, I see why that comment, discussion, way of looking at things, could be helpful."

In this exchange with Brad I had no rationale to fit this into my therapeutic puzzle. Normally I would sit with a student and help them "Understand" their upset so they could feel differently about it.

Being guided has nothing to do with being rational, at least not in the sense that we normally think about rational. Once you've experienced Inner Guidance then it actually is very rational to continue to approach things using that guidance.

This experience meant that I could actually throw out my long held model of helping my students. Wait a minute, it meant I could throw out my long held model of how I live life. WOW!

I wish I could tell you that after that experience with Brad my life became one of pure awakened guidance. Instead, it has been a steady beautiful march towards self-awareness. As of this writing I certainly spend more of my time aware of my Inner Guidance then ever before and I expect that awareness to continue to grow.

You may not have experienced the type of connection with your Inner Guide that I describe in my story with Brad. But, many people experience Guidance when they are involved in some activity that occupies their awareness completely such as music, art or sports. Musicians, artists or athletes describe being "In the Zone." Their mind is so occupied with what they are doing that they create pieces of art or athletic feats that dazzle. This is of course not limited to artists and athletes, it can include surgeons and someone crocheting on their couch at home and almost any activity that allows us to let go of our ego.

There is a lot of wonderful information in the world that helps people resolve difficulties in their lives. This includes difficulties of a physical nature such as a flat tire or psychological difficulties such as depression. I have certainly used many forms of information to improve my life in many, many ways. But, there is no information, technology, or method that has helped me with my difficulties with the certitude and clarity of my Inner Guide.

If you are regularly making a conscious connection with your Inner Guidance, you will shift your life dramatically. For me this has meant that I continue to take advantage of all that wonderful worldly information to improve my life, but I know that in the end my Inner Guidance trumps them all. My hope and belief is that one day I will be able to rely completely on my Inner Guide. Based on my life experience of increasing connection with my Inner Guide it certainly looks like I am headed in that direction.

In the following chapters I will describe techniques that will help you clear your mind so that you can consciously choose to connect with your Inner Guidance. This clarity of mind will allow you to live "In the Zone" all the time, Living the Guided Life.

Although most people have an awareness of their intuitive side (Inner Guidance) it still seems mysterious and distant from their every day experience. Part 1 of Living the Guided Life includes chapters 1-4 and will help you to understand your Inner Guidance in a way that will help you recognize its accessibility.

Part 2, Undoing Your Blocks to Inner Guidance, includes Chapters 5-9 and is designed to help you recognize and release your blocks to Inner Guidance.

Part three, Choice as a Key to Inner Guidance, includes chapter 10-14 and raises your awareness of the idea that you choose your thoughts. With this increased awareness you will learn to make choices that enhance contact with your Inner Guide.

Part 4, Redefining You to Connect with Inner Guidance, includes Chapters 15-20 and will help you understand how to think about yourself in such a way as to broaden your awareness of your Inner Guide.

At the end of each chapter you will find the "Toolbox of ideas for Inner Guidance." The "Toolbox" at the end of each chapter will include the ideas from the previous chapters and one from the current chapter. The design of the "Toolbox" is purposeful in that it builds on itself. Each idea is independently very powerful, but when looked at, and understood in their entirety they can transform your communication with your Inner Guide.

You may encounter some words or terms that you don't understand or they seem to be used in a way you are not used to. Please check the Clarification of Terms at the end of the book as a reference if something seems to not make sense.

Toolbox of ideas for Inner Guidance

1. Inner guidance trumps any other guidance.

Chapter 2
SPEAKING INNER GUIDE

Defining Inner Guidance

As you embark on this process of Living the Guided Life defining Inner Guidance is helpful. In this way you will have an idea of what it is that you are seeking to achieve.

Most people have experienced moments in their lives where they simply, "Knew" how to handle something in any particular moment. It is this "Knowing" that we are working to contact more regularly. There is no need to figure anything out, you just "Know" what to do or say next. This awareness can be called by many names. Some might call it intuition, higher self, higher mind, higher power, spirit or even divinity.

I refer to this level of awareness as Inner Guidance. My belief is that everyone has this Inner Guidance available to them. I use the term Inner Guidance because it is neutral, in that all of the definitions in the previous paragraph can be applied to Inner Guidance. It comes from inside of us (our thinking) and it guides us. In the end it does not matter what you call this Guidance, the only thing that matters is that you believe (even just a little bit) that it is accessible to you. Once you have even a 1% belief in this Inner Guidance, and you acknowledge that belief, you can begin to expand your awareness of it.

I leave it to you to decide how you would like to define this Inner Guidance. As you read on you will encounter the term Inner Guidance and Inner Guide repeatedly and I believe you will find that it applies to any of the definitions from above: Intuition, The Zone, Higher Self, Higher Mind, Higher Power, Spirit, or Divinity.

To endeavor to live the Guided Life means that you are seeking more regular contact with your Inner Guidance

Learning to "Speak" Inner Guide

If you speak English and are moving to a small village in the south of France, you can enhance your experience in that village by learning some French. In fact, in order to take full advantage of life in that village, you should probably do some research on the culture and priorities of the people in that village. All of this will make your experience in this foreign land richer and more enjoyable.

The same holds true for learning to communicate with your Inner Guide. The clarity and richness of your connection with your Inner Guide can be enhanced by understanding your Inner Guide. We live in a world that is, for the most part, unaware of the language of Inner Guidance. Most people in the world are not aware of, or have a limited connection to true Inner Guidance. Therefore we are all living in a land that does not speak that language.

If you are reading this book you probably would like to take a peaceful, enjoyable trip to the world of your Inner Guide. Of course everyone would like to take this trip. It is just that some people are more aware of this desire than others. In order to make this trip successful, you must learn about the language and culture of Inner Guidance. In this way you will be able to take full advantage of all that your Inner Guide has to offer.

What *does* your Inner Guide Have to Offer?

Your Inner Guide is pure peace and unconditional love. Wow, that is short sweet and simple. Alright, let's pack our bags and head off on that trip. Okay, don't start packing yet, although it is that simple, we have tended to make things very complicated in this unguided world. Unfortunately, for most of us just the identification of the qualities of our Inner Guide is not enough to open up our awareness to the Guidance.

Remember, in order to understand a foreign language, and receiving regular Inner Guidance is foreign to most folks, you must learn to speak and live that language. This means that you must learn to live peacefully and lovingly. To offer the verbal rhetoric of peace and love is not enough. One must be living these principles in order for the communication lines to fully open up.

Your Inner Guide is pure, completely peaceful and unconditionally loving. These are qualities that most of us cannot identify with, let alone live, even some of the time. But there are qualities that mirror the qualities of our Inner Guide's that seem more manageable and attainable. These include patience, non-judgment, and acceptance. These life skills are like stops or sign posts on the journey to pure peace and unconditional love. Before I can get to France I need to get to the airport. Before I can get to pure peaceful unconditional love I must work on being more patient, non-judgmental and accepting. That is the process of learning to match the language or frequency of your Inner Guide in order to expand your awareness of your Inner Guidance. For clarity sake, I want you to realize that for most people, including myself, the journey to peace is usually a process of growing awareness, not an instantaneous experience.

At this point the following question may have occurred to you: Why must I match the language or frequency of my Inner Guide, why doesn't it match mine? Good for you, this is an excellent question and bears some examination.

Why Can't My Inner Guide match my frequency or speak my Language?

One of the qualities of your Inner Guide that I listed earlier was purity. Your Inner Guide is pure in its thoughts. In other words it does not allow any outside influences to veer it off its path of peace and love. I think we can all acknowledge that we occasionally veer of into an un-loving, unpeaceful thought. If we expected our Inner Guide to match our language or frequency we would be asking it to give up its purity. We would be asking it to have an occasional unloving, un-peaceful, impure thought. I don't know about you but I want my Guidance to remain pure.

Our Inner Guide is exceptional in that, although it understands our struggles, it does not buy into them (it remains pure). That makes it uniquely capable of helping us out of our struggles.

A terrific analogy for this pure guidance is a foreign language teacher. You would like a foreign language teacher who can speak the language you want to learn perfectly. Additionally, he can understand you and instantly identify your flaws and tell you how to correct them, but does not allow your imperfections to influence his perfection. We would not want a teacher who helps us correct our grammar but in the process begins to pick up some of our flaws, and therefore becomes a flawed teacher.

Toolbox of ideas for Inner Guidance

1. Inner Guidance trumps any other guidance.
2. Learning the language of Inner Guidance takes practice like learning a foreign language. Your Inner Guide is pure.

Chapter 3
INNER GUIDE RADIO

As you embark on the journey of Living the Guided Life it is important to understand how your Inner Guide broadcasts its message of peace.

Your Inner Guide's expertise on peace and love is always being broadcast, like a radio station. You can tune your radio to various stations with the simple turn of a dial or more recently with the push of a button. As you change the stations with the push of a button you are changing the frequency that your radio is picking up.

When you are not hearing the broadcast of a particular station it is not because they are not sending out their signal on their designated frequency. It is because you have chosen to listen to another station broadcasting at another frequency. All those other stations continue to broadcast, even when you are not tuned into their frequency.

This is also true for your Inner Guide. It is always broadcasting its signal of peace and love. You are simply choosing to listen to a different frequency when you do not hear the guidance.

You might ask, "Why doesn't my Inner Guide just impose its broadcast upon me?" Because attack of any kind is not loving. If your Inner

Guide stepped in and interfered with the broadcast you are choosing to listen to, it would be engaging in a form of attack. Just like the villains in some of our most popular movies who break into national television broadcasts in order to give their demands. Being pure unconditional love your Inner Guide cannot do that.

Your Inner Guide will simply allow you to listen to whatever broadcast you choose to. When you choose to listen to its broadcast it will share its guidance with you.

Toolbox of ideas for Inner Guidance

1. Inner Guidance trumps any other guidance.

2. Learning the language of Inner Guidance takes practice like learning a foreign language. Your Inner Guide is pure.

3. Your Inner Guide is **ALWAYS** broadcasting its message of peace. You need only to tune in.

Chapter 4

INNER GUIDE AS PEACEFUL GUIDE

Another question that has probably occurred to you is: Why doesn't my internal guide simply take over my thinking and shift it to pure unconditional love? You are excellent, that is a very good question, which also bears some examination.

Since understanding unconditional love is a key to answering this question let's start this examination with a detailed look at it.

Love is an experience and therefore hard to describe with words. But we will do our best here. First of all, unconditional love is not what we hear about in our general day to day experience. We hear and see people in love with one another for all kinds of reasons such as physical attraction, common interests, feeling safe, and a plethora of other reasons.

Love, with no conditions, means there is no reason, I just love. It does not matter what is happening anywhere or how anyone else is behaving, I just experience love all the time. Very few people have this experience of love, even sometimes. True pure unconditional love seems to be beyond our limited awareness.

Most of us don't think or feel in this expanded way. The feeling we call "Love" is usually contingent on someone or something else behaving in a certain way. When this person or thing doesn't behave in a way that we find acceptable we get angry and we don't feel love.

You will remember from the previous chapter that another quality of unconditional love is that it never attacks. This makes sense. To attack would not be loving so unconditional love would be incapable of that experience.

Remember, we are working to match the language or **frequency** of our Inner Guide. If we experience dissatisfaction or even disagreement with someone else's behavior or thinking, we are thinking in an unloving and non-peaceful way. Any thought that I should "impose" my way of thinking or doing upon another is a form of attack. Attack in any form is not pure, unconditional love.

I am not suggesting that you should be able to live a life without any experience of dissatisfaction or disagreement. But, we can continually work to diminish the level of disagreement and/or dissatisfaction in our lives. In this way we are working towards greater connection with our Inner Guidance. This is like our Inner Guide Radio analogy. By carefully choosing your thoughts you are fine tuning your receiver.

Here is how your Inner Guide handles someone who might disagree with it or not be willing to listen to its guidance (advice). Remember, being only pure unconditional love your Inner Guide can't impose its belief system or guidance upon anyone. Therefore, it quietly and patiently waits until one is willing to listen, then it shares its guidance. In this way the guidance/advice is not experienced as an imposition, it is experienced as the fulfillment of ones desire or request for that guidance.

This helps to answer the question from above, "Why doesn't my Inner Guide just take over my thinking and shift it to unconditionally loving thoughts?" Your Inner Guide is not capable of taking over your thinking. A "take over" would be considered a form of attack, and being pure unconditional love your Inner Guide is incapable of any form of attack.

Mirroring Unconditional Love through patience

One of the ways we can practice mirroring or matching the language or frequency of our Inner Guide is to notice a moment when we find ourselves believing that someone else needs to do something differently or think about something differently.

For instance, you might hear someone being chauvinistic, racist or judgmental in some way shape or form. If you fancy yourself an enlightened being you might feel the need to get that person to look on the situation or person in a more loving light. But again, this attempt to impose your belief system upon them will invariably be interpreted as an attack. Instead, match the language and frequency of your Inner Guide. Sit back and know that someday this person will be ready to hear about a loving way to look at the situation or person and you will "know" (via Guidance) when they are ready and you will share.

Let's take this story a step further. You are spending regular time with this acquaintance who is being chauvinist or racist. His experience is that his judgments are regularly met with resistance, attack and upset. You on the other hand are a person in his life who seems unaffected. In fact you are the person who listens and seems to have little to no judgment about him and what he shares. At some point your acceptance will dawn on your acquaintance. This dawning may not be conscious. You will then be ready to pounce like a Tiger and attack him!! No, just kidding. He will be ready to open up to you, knowing that you will not judge him. You have now created an opportunity to guide someone else along the path to peace and love by being peace and love yourself.

I am sure you agree that we generally don't experience unconditional love, loving everyone and everything for no reason and with no exceptions. This brings me to the conclusion that we actually don't really *know* (are not able to easily access) the experience of unconditional love. That doesn't mean that there aren't people out there that do experience unconditional love. I believe there are.

I also know that many of you have had moments in your lives where you have had an expanded awareness and have touched into the experience of unconditional love. But, I believe there are few of us who are living the experience of unconditional love regularly, let alone always.

The above story about our judgmental acquaintance is an excellent example of matching the frequency of loving thoughts that define our Inner Guide. Through experiences such as this we get more comfortable with the foreign language of Inner Guidance.

Funny thing is, as we sit back and work to not impose our beliefs on another by not judging them, we are matching another of our Inner Guide's frequencies: Peace. Remember we described our Inner Guide and its language as pure, unconditionally loving, and peaceful. Listening to someone with a viewpoint that does not match up with my own and having no need to get them to change, I experience a much more peaceful state of mind. Whereas, when I feel the need to convince someone to think like I do, I get agitated, frustrated or maybe just mildly annoyed. None of these ways of feeling and thinking match up with my Inner Guide's frequency/language.

You will know that you are on your way to sharing from a place of love when people not agreeing with you brings up no upsetting feelings. You will know you are sharing from Inner Guidance when love is your experience even when someone disagrees with you. These last two sentences present an important distinction. It is a wonderful thing to experience little to no upsetting feelings. It is entirely different to experience love. Experiencing less and less upsetting feelings is a signpost on the path to experiencing pure love.

Reflections of Inner Guidance

Purity, unconditional love and 24/7 peace of mind are not regular experiences in this world. But, I wrote earlier that there are some experiences in this world that reflect or mirror those concepts. Some of these are patience, non-judgment and acceptance. What I really mean to say here is: Becoming more patient, less judgmental and more accepting. If one was purely non-judgmental, completely patient and completely accepting they would no longer need Inner Guidance they would *be* Inner Guidance.

One of the ways we set ourselves up for failure in this process is by setting unattainable standards. If you expect yourself to show up as unconditionally loving you are probably setting yourself up to be disappointed. There are few of us that can show up that way even sometimes. But, we can all become more and more accepting and less and less judgmental and in the process we will become more and more loving. This is like the adage, "Progress not perfection." Expect yourself to make progress. Don't expect yourself to be perfect.

The earlier story of listening to a person share judgments and struggles and practicing patience and non-judgment with them is not always easy to do. You may have even had the thought, "That's great to listen to someone without judging them, but I find that very difficult." That is a regular experience in this world, "I want to be more patient and less judgmental but when it comes down to the moment when I have the opportunity to practice these ways of being, I find it very difficult."

My student Julie would often arrive at school before me. 3 to 4 times a week I would find her sitting outside my office door first thing in the morning waiting to talk with me and/or our school social worker Barbara about something that had upset her. These stories often revolved around boys. She had had sex with multiple partners the night before. She thought she was pregnant. She was worried her boyfriend would find out she cheated on him. She was worried she had a sexually transmitted disease. She had gotten drunk, blacked out and thought maybe she had been raped. She was worried her boyfriend had cheated on her and the list went on and on. Of course she also had the more typical teenage issues to discuss as well: fights with family members, concerns about her grades, peer pressure, drug use etcetera.

Having Julie as a student was one of my opportunities to practice patience, less judgment, and more acceptance. As Julie would come in day after day having repeated the same mistakes and with many of the same concerns, I had to frequently remind myself that being in a peaceful non judgmental state of mind was the best way for me to help her. By staying peaceful I could be guided as to what to say to help Julie.

Julie and her family acknowledged that Julie made more progress during her school year in our program than at any other point in her life. At the end of the school year Julie offered the following.

"The best thing about this school year was being able to talk with Chris and Barbara about my struggles. They would just listen to me and give me feedback on my decisions. Everyone else always acted so shocked or felt sorry for me when I would tell them my stories. But Chris and Barbara would just sit and listen and didn't seem to ever be upset or to feel sorry for me. They wouldn't tell me what I should do, they would just ask me what I wanted and then help me to get what I wanted." Julie had never mentioned this appreciation for Barbara and my approach to her before. It was affirmation that listening to people with as little judgment as possible offers them a space of love to grow and change if that is what they desire. When someone feels accepted no matter what, they are much more likely to open up as well as listen. Our accepting attitude towards Julie allowed us to have a greater level of influence with her.

We would listen and ask what Julie wanted and then give her feedback on her choices. In this way our advice was experienced by Julie as the fulfillment of her request for help, rather than the imposition of our values upon her.

As you can imagine it wasn't always easy for me to remain nonjudgmental about Julie's experiences. It is often difficult for anyone to practice acceptance, less judgment and patience with others let alone with ourselves. In chapters 6 and 7 we will examine why it is difficult to practice these ways of being that mirror the frequency of our Inner Guide.

Toolbox of ideas for Inner Guidance

1. Inner Guidance trumps any other guidance.

2. Learning the language of Inner Guidance takes practice like learning a foreign language. Your Inner Guide is pure.

3. Your Inner Guide is **ALWAYS** broadcasting its message of peace. You need only to tune in.

4. Patience, less judgment and acceptance are mindsets that help you to match the frequency of your Inner Guide.

Part 2

UNDOING YOUR BLOCKS TO INNER GUIDANCE

_____ *Chapter 5* _____

SUCCESSES AND FAILURES

No matter where you are in your process of tapping into your Inner Guidance, there are a number of ideas and techniques that will help you expand your connection to that guidance. That means, if you are almost completely unaware of your Inner Guidance or you have been tapping into it for years your connection can be expanded.

If we are successful, or if we fail at a certain task, by paying attention to the process that brought us to the success or failure we can become better at that task. In other words if I understand what contributed to my failure I can avoid that in the future. If I notice what contributed to my success I can do more of that and increase my successful experiences.

In the process of expanding my awareness of Inner Guidance I often did not understand or realize what was happening to me. Not until I looked back on it and spent some time figuring out "What just happened?", or "What exactly has happened to me over the last 20 years?" By looking back I could identify what happened to help me expand my awareness, and what hindered me.

This idea of learning from your failures and your successes is no re-velatory message. We have all had some level of success in some areas of our lives and we probably experienced that success in part by noticing what worked and what didn't. This process also holds true for tapping into your Inner Guidance.

Pay attention to those experiences that have engendered guidance for you and work to "Repeat Often." As well, notice those "Experiences" that engender a disconnection from guidance, a feeling of being lost and not knowing what to do. Avoid those "Experiences."

It is important here to delineate my distinction for "Experience" in the above paragraph. I don't mean the events that occur to you in your life. By "Experience" I mean how you experience what happens in your life, or how you think about the people and events in your life and your subsequent feelings. By the way, "Experience" (as I am defining it), is one of the rungs on the Responsibility Ladder mentioned in chapter 1.

With that distinction for "Experience" in mind let's look at the above paragraph again.

Pay attention to those experiences (ways of thinking and subse-quent feelings) that have engendered guidance for you and work to "Repeat Often." As well, notice those "Experiences" (ways of thinking and subsequent feelings) that engender a disconnection from guid-ance, a feeling of being lost and not knowing what to do. Avoid those "Experiences" (ways of thinking and subsequent feelings).

As you will find out in the pages that follow, how you think about yourself and life in general (how you experience yourself and life in general) is the key to expanding the connection you have with your Inner Guide.

Toolbox of ideas for Inner Guidance

1. Inner guidance trumps any other guidance.

2. Learning the language of Inner Guidance takes practice like learning a foreign language. Your Inner Guide is pure.

3. Your Inner Guide is **ALWAYS** broadcasting its message of peace. You need only to tune in.

4. Patience, less judgment and acceptance are mindsets that help you to match the frequency of your Inner Guide.

5. Pay attention to what thoughts bring you closer to Inner Guidance and repeat them as often as possible.

Chapter 6
UNLEARNING WHAT
YOU HAVE LEARNED

Part of the difficulty in matching the frequency of our Inner Guide is that we have grown up learning the frequency of judgment, impatience and non-acceptance. With this in mind Yoda, the Jedi Master from the Star Wars movies was right when he told Luke Skywalker, "You must unlearn what you have learned."

In order to become fluent in a foreign language one of the things that must happen is that we must unlearn some of the ways of our native language. This is true when learning the language of Inner Guidance as well. The native language of this world is very clearly judgment, impatience and non-acceptance. You need only look around and listen to your fellow man to realize this.

French and English can co-exist in your mind and you can tap into either when you choose. If you are a native English speaker learning French, the new French language does not displace English. It sits along side of it. At this point you can choose which language you will speak. If you immerse yourself in the French language, perhaps you take up permanent residence in that French village, your English will eventually begin to fade into the background.

Before being introduced to a foreign language you are ignorant of its way of communicating. There are some similarities with learning the language of Inner Guidance. At first you are not aware of a less judgmental way to think about things. But once you have been introduced to the idea that you can think about life with less judgment you have reached a point where you have the choices in your mind. You can choose to have judgments about this event or person or you can choose to have acceptance of it/them. Knowing that each way of thinking will lead to either a decrease or an increase in your peace of mind and therefore your connection with Inner Guidance

At first it is difficult to think in less judgmental terms. But, with more and more practice and immersion it becomes less of a task and more natural. The judgmental part of your mind starts to fade into the background just as your native English will fade into the background as you live in that French village and speak only French.

You are, "Unlearning what you have learned." Recognizing that I have a choice about whether I am judgmental or accepting is one of those signposts along the path to Inner Guidance. It is progress from the place where most people experience life as a series of personal judgments and they don't realize they can choose not to judge and receive Guidance instead.

Since so much of this process of growing your connection with Inner Guidance revolves around letting go of judgments, this would be a good time to examine judgments. Wow, imagine that, the next chapter just happens to be about Judgments, how lucky are you?

Toolbox of ideas for Inner Guidance

1. Inner guidance trumps any other guidance.

2. Learning the language of Inner Guidance takes practice like learning a foreign language. Your Inner Guide is pure.

3. Your Inner Guide is **ALWAYS** broadcasting its message of peace. You need only to tune in.

4. Patience, less judgment and acceptance are mindsets that help you to match the frequency of your Inner Guide.

5. Pay attention to what thoughts bring you closer to Inner Guidance and repeat them as often as possible.

6. You must unlearn the language of judgment and learn the language of acceptance.

Chapter 7
JUDGMENTS, MINE
OR INNER GUIDES?

To Judge or not to Judge that is the Question

A judgment is essentially one's opinion about a thing, an event or a person. For simplicity sake we generally put things, events and people into one of two categories - good/right or bad/wrong. We can view a person/event/thing as good one day and bad the next based on our perception changing.

Viewing events, people, or things as good or bad is based entirely on the opinion of the observer. Two people can go through the same experience, one can think the experience is wonderful and the other can think the experience is awful.

An example of this is two students receiving "B" grades on a research paper in their 12th grade English class. One student is a straight "A" student. The other student is a straight "D" student. You can imagine the straight "A" student would be disappointed in a B grade while the D student would be excited about the B grade. They are both going through the same event, earning a B grade. But, their experience (thinking and subsequent feelings) of the event is different.

You and I could sit for hours coming up with an extensive list of stories like our high school students in the previous paragraph. There is a never ending list of examples of people having varying perceptions/experiences of the same person/event/thing.

This idea of two people having different experiences of the same event helps me understand an important concept. How I experience (think and feel about) an event, person or thing does not come from the event, person or thing. That's right, don't touch that dial. I just wrote that events, people and things don't dictate our experience (thoughts and feelings). Our thinking is what determines our experience of everything.

I believe this because there are no events, people or things that everyone experiences exactly the same. If we could come up with any event, person or thing that all people had the exact same experience (thoughts/feelings) of, I would say the experience comes from the event, thing or person itself. But there are no people, events or things that all humans experience exactly the same. Therefore the experience is coming from the people.

I have found that one of the best ways for me to let go of my judgments is to go back to a technique I wrote about in chapter 5. Look back at what has and has not worked. When I take a look back at my life I certainly have had judgments about the things, events and people that I experienced.

One event or time in my life in particular stands out for me as one that I mistakenly judged as awful.

When I was 16 years old my older brother Jeff, who was an alcoholic and drug addict, was convicted of drug trafficking and spent 18 months in the Ohio State Penitentiary. At the time, I was concerned about Jeff's well-being and I was embarrassed that a family member was convicted of a crime. No one could have convinced me that this was in any way good.

It turns out this jail sentence was one of the best things that ever happened to my brother. His experience in jail was so painful that when he got out he was determined to change his life. He got sober, ending 15 years of addictive and criminal behavior. He got his GED and in a few years earned a masters degree in Social Work and began a career helping others.

This is a classic example of an event looking awful but in retrospect it was wonderful. I can look back on many events in my life and realize that my initial judgment about them was incorrect. The following is a Chinese parable that elucidates the same idea.

"Long ago, there was a farmer who lived in China. This was a poor farmer who had but one horse. He used his horse to plow the fields so that he could make a living. One day, the horse ran away. "Oh no!" cried the neighbors, "That is terrible!" The old farmer shrugged and said: "Good news, bad news – who knows."

Several days later, the farmer's horse returned to the farm with several wild horses following behind. The farmer and his son managed to capture the horses, all of them of great beauty. "Oh, how wonderful!" cried the neighbors. Once again, the farmer simply shrugged and said: "Good news, bad news – who knows."

The next day, the farmer's twenty-year-old-son managed to capture one of the wild horses, but while attempting to break the steed, was thrown and his leg was badly broken. The neighbors rushed over, peering at the young man in bed. "Oh, this is awful news!" they cried. The farmer shrugged, "Good news, bad news, who knows?"

A few weeks later, the Chinese army came by, conscripting all the area's young men for war raging in the south. They couldn't take the young man with the broken leg. The neighbors said, "Farmer you are so lucky that your son did not get taken to fight in the war." To which the farmer replied, "Good news, bad news, who knows?"

Take a few moments right now and look back on some of the events in your life. You should be able to identify similar events that seemed awful at the time and in the end turned out okay or even wonderful. We can also look back on some events that we thought were wonderful that turned out to be awful. Of course we can also identify those experiences where it turned out exactly as we judged. But let's be honest, how often have things turned out exactly as you judged they would?

Let's now examine the experience of our past judgments in the vein of what works and what does not work. How often does your judgment about things, events and people turn out to be correct? If you are being honest you will probably realize that your ability to judge what is good or bad or how events will work out is limited at best.

Most people have a field in which they have had extensive training and therefore are better judges within that field than most people. For instance a doctor will do a much better job of judging the type, extent and treatment of an illness than a lay person. They can look at the medical situation and make a much more informed judgment.

Problem is, our entire lives are spent navigating the world of inter-personal relationships with limited training, which leads to poor judgment in that area of our life.

Intermittent Reinforcement of Our Judgments

The world offers us intermittent reinforcement of the idea that we can judge what is best for ourselves and others. Intermittent reinforcement as a psychological term describes having successes sometimes, which causes me to continue the behavior. Psychologists have found that intermittent reinforcement is one of the most powerful methods for continuing a behavior. In other words I experience that my judgments are correct every once in a while so I continue to rely on my judgments, even though there might be another source of information that would do a better job.

My cat Buddy used to roam far and wide around our neighborhood. My wife and I would go out of town frequently and we would need to get Buddy into the house before we left. Using intermittent reinforcement, I developed a technique for getting Buddy back inside.

He loved canned food and I started honking an old fashioned bike horn whenever I would give him canned food (2 or 3 times a week). After just a few weeks of this I could honk the horn outside our front or back door and within a minute Buddy would come running inside anticipating some canned food. After this initial training period I only gave Buddy the canned food after honking the horn on an intermittent basis.

At this point Buddy was trained that the bike horn meant canned food. Not every time mind you. If at some point I no longer gave Buddy the canned food after honking the horn he would continue to respond to the horn as if he was going to get canned food. In fact the intermittent reinforcement schedule meant that it would take quite a long time before Buddy would give up on the horn equaling canned food idea. In his mind the intermittent nature of the reinforcement lead him to think, "Will I get it this time?" and he would keep coming back.

Most people have the same experience with their judgments. They are periodically correct (reinforced) so they keep going back to them (judgments). Who are the people that often make the most dramatic changes in their lives? Those who have reached a "Bottom". They recognize that their judgments are not working. The classic example of this is the alcoholic or drug addict who finally admits that they have a problem.

My brother Jeff is a great example of this. My family tried to help Jeff in myriad ways before he ended up in jail. Jeff believed on some level that he could figure things out and make life okay using his own judgments. For those of us who knew Jeff his judgments were clearly askew. After becoming sober he would tell the following story about his flawed judgment while his addiction was active.

"I was constantly getting in trouble. To me it looked like cars were the problem. I would get arrested for driving drunk, crash a car, get my license suspended and on and on. I had the realization that cars were the cause of all my problems. So, I decided to get a moped. I would use that as my mode of transportation and my problems would be solved. I didn't need to stop using and selling drugs and alcohol I just needed to drive a moped!!"

Now that is beautiful example of some skewed judgment. It was not until Jeff reached his bottom, living in a 6 x 8 jail cell for 18 months that he decided his assessment (judgment/thinking) about things must not be working. He was ready to listen to another source of information for what was best for him.

The question is: When will you be ready to stop relying on your judgments and allow your Inner Guidance to direct your life? Will it take a jail sentence, a divorce, a miserable job situation, or some other painful experience? Or, are you ready to start receiving that Inner Guidance right now?

The fact is, you will be ready once you acknowledge, "I don't know" what is best for me!!

Toolbox of ideas for Inner Guidance

1. Inner guidance trumps any other guidance.

2. Learning the language of Inner Guidance takes practice like learning a foreign language. Your Inner Guide is pure.

3. Your Inner Guide is **ALWAYS** broadcasting its message of peace. You need only to tune in.

4. Patience, less judgment and acceptance are mindsets that help you to match the frequency of your Inner Guide.

5. Pay attention to what thoughts bring you closer to Inner Guidance and repeat them as often as possible.

6. You must unlearn the language of judgment and learn the language of acceptance.

7. Your Inner Guide is the best judge of what is good for you!!

Chapter 8
I DON'T KNOW

Not Knowing, To Receive Guidance or The "I don't Know" Mind

When my brother Jeff came out of Jail he told my parents he wanted to go to college. My parents told him they would pay for college if he agreed to go to a rehab center for 60 days first. These kinds of offers had been made many times in the past. Jeff had turned them all down. At this point Jeff realized that he needed a new view and perspective on things if he was to straighten out his life. He agreed to my parent's terms.

Jeff called from the rehab center a week later and told my parents where he had bags of cocaine and Quaaludes hidden in their home and asked them to flush them down the toilet. He never used drugs or alcohol again.

Jeff had gotten to the "I don't know" mind. He recognized that his judgment was getting him nowhere. "I don't know what is best for me." He was then willing to listen to others about what might help him. He told many stories about staff members and fellow addicts at the rehab center giving him sage advice that helped him stay sober. He also made it clear that he had heard many of these things before, but now was willing to listen and use the advice.

Two things were occurring here for Jeff. One, he became willing to listen to those around him about what was best for him because he realized his own judgment wasn't working. Two, his Inner Guide was communicating to him through others. As Jeff recognized, he had been hearing many of these ideas before but chose not to act on them. Meaning, his Inner Guide's broadcast was always steering him toward peace of mind. He just wasn't tuned in. By reaching the "I don't know" mind he was able to tune into his Inner Guidance. It just happened to be broadcasting through the people around him.

Being clever you are probably asking the question, "What's with this 'I don't know mind'?" "Why can't I "know" and receive guidance?" Excellent questions that again bear some examination.

You probably know someone who shows up like a know-it-all. I certainly have some people in my life that show up that way. Have you ever tried to tell/explain/teach something to a Know It All. Have you noticed that "Know It Alls" are unwilling to listen to what other people have to say? For whatever reason, it is important to the Know-It-All that they appear smart or knowledgeable to others and to themselves. When this is important to someone they are less willing to learn from others.

This idea of needing to show up as knowledgeable runs on a con-tinuum. 1 is having a closed mind and being completely unwilling to listen to the ideas of others. 10 is having set aside all my judgments and allowing my Inner Guide to direct me. The higher you can move up on this scale the more open you will be to your Inner Guidance.

Yet another way of explaining this idea is to think about how little a Know-It-All is able to learn because of their closed mind. If we agree that that is the case, "Know It Alls" have trouble learning from others because their minds are closed, then we must look at the other extreme.

I think that the opposite is also true, if I can decide that, "I know nothing", my Inner Guide can teach me everything.

Now at this point we need to define "Everything." Because our ego will immediately leap on this assertion and ask the question, "Doesn't being taught everything mean that I would know-it-all?" The answer is no. Because your Inner Guide has a different definition for "Everything" than does your ego.

Your Inner Guide's definition of "Everything" is "Peace of Mind." Your Inner Guide can Guide you through any experience and help to make it peaceful and fulfilling. This occurs in part because that is your Inner Guide's singular purpose. To bring you peace and help you live a more loving life. Your ego has many other varied goals therefore the understanding you get from your ego will steer you toward these other goals that may conflict with your peace of mind.

One of your ego's goals is looking good or looking better than others. With that as a goal the idea of "knowing everything" looks very appealing. How much better would you look than everyone else if you knew Everything. Under these circumstances Everything is the accumulation of knowledge to look better than others. As you can see, the two definitions of everything lead to very different lives. One dominated by the accumulation of information to look better than others, the other focused on peace of mind.

Getting to the "I don't know" mind means that I have let go of my judgments. This releasing of my judgments is a process of incrementally moving up on the continuum, not instantaneous release of all judgments. I am releasing the idea that I know what is best or what is worse for me or anyone else.

Your Inner Guide's purpose is your well-being, happiness and peace of mind. Its guidance revolves around whether an idea will bring you greater peace. Being pure peace and unconditional love your Inner Guide is an expert in this area. When that part of me that I call my ego believes that it knows what is best for me it essentially blocks my Inner

Guide's broadcast. You can now see why it is so important to get to the "I don't know" mind.

We can also revisit the idea of Inner Guide Radio at this point. Judgment is one of the broadcasts we choose to listen to instead of Inner Guidance. Judgment is of the intellect and the ego. Getting to the "I don't know" mind is one of the techniques for tuning in more precisely to the broadcast of your Inner Guide. "I Don't Know", means that you have let go of judgments. Then your Inner Guide's broadcast will more clearly enter your awareness because you have cleared the way to hear it.

This is why people who have hit bottom often seem to have miraculous changes occur in their lives. They have completely and entirely recognized (not necessarily consciously) that they don't know what is best for them. They have cleared the way to hear their Inner Guide's broadcast. When they do this they are guided toward actions that help them live more loving and peaceful lives.

I am sure you have experienced this release of judgments and connected with your Inner Guide's wisdom. Have you ever laid down to sleep or nap and you remember something that you have been searching your mind for during your waking hours. Most people have had that experience or gotten a great idea just as they are drifting off to sleep. What happened in these moments is that you have let go of all your concerns, worries or judgments. Your mind has relaxed and stopped searching for answers. In that relaxed peaceful state you dialed into the broadcast of your Inner Guide.

Toolbox of ideas for Inner Guidance

1. Inner guidance trumps any other guidance.

2. Learning the language of Inner Guidance takes practice like learning a foreign language. Your Inner Guide is pure.

3. Your Inner Guide is **ALWAYS** broadcasting its message of peace. You need only to tune in.

4. Pay attention to what thoughts bring you closer to Inner Guidance and repeat them as often as possible.

5. Pay attention to what thoughts bring you closer to Inner Guidance and repeat them as often as possible.

6. You must unlearn the language of judgment and learn the language of acceptance.

7. Your Inner Guide is the best judge of what is good for you!!

8. Acknowledging that you "Don't Know" what is best for you, opens you up to your Inner Guidance that does "Know" what is best for you.

Chapter 9
THE SUBCONSCIOUS MIND

That the two phases of the mind are related can be well illustrated by comparing the conscious mind with a sponge, and the subconscious with the water permeating the sponge. We know that every fiber of the sponge is in touch with the water, and in the same manner, every part of the conscious mind, as well as every atom in the personality is in touch with the subconscious, and completely filled, through and through, with the life and the force of the subconscious.

Christian D. Larson, Your Forces and How To Use Them

The subtitle to Living the Guided Life is: A Path to Conscious Connection with Your Inner Guide. I am laying out a path for making a conscious choice to hear your Inner Guide's broadcast, rather than just randomly tuning into the broadcast at unspecified times and places. Christian Larson points out the difficulty in making any conscious choices in that our subconscious influences all aspects of personhood. We must understand our subconscious mind so that we can effect it and therefore effect our conscious choices.

Our examination of the subconscious mind will begin with a look at the subconscious mind's preoccupation with the past.

The Past as my Guide or Inner Guidance?

In order to further recognize how our judgments interfere with tuning into our Inner Guide's broadcast we must understand the broadcast we are choosing to listen to. Since we can't push a button to listen to Inner Guidance, we will need to make a conscious choice to listen to it. Greater understanding of the various broadcasts we can listen to helps us make that conscious choice.

The primary frequency 90% or more of people listen to, 90% or more of the time, is the past. You are mostly choosing to tune into the past as your guidance for the future. This is one of the broadcasts that interfere with Inner Guidance. Inner Guidance that provides information that is vastly superior to what your intellect or ego can provide by reviewing the past. This may be a difficult concept to accept, but once you have made decisions based on Inner Guidance you will no longer question this assertion. In chapter 15 "Personal Responsibility" I describe how you will experience intellectual decisions based on the past and Guided decisions very differently.

When I judge that I know, based on the broadcast from the past, what is best for me, I am unable to pick up on what my Inner Guide thinks is best for me, being broadcast on the "Present" frequency. I am choosing to listen to a broadcast other than my Inner Guide's. Therefore in order to match my Inner Guide's frequency I must learn to tune out of the past and into the present.

I wrote earlier that we should take time to review what has worked and what has not worked so that we can repeat more of what works. There is a fine line here between reviewing the past for what has worked and reviewing the past to avoid living in the present moment.

Yes, we can learn from the past, but we do not want to obsess about the past or feel sad, angry, disappointed, etcetera about the past. None of those ways of being are matching the frequency of peace, love and joy that our Inner Guide is broadcasting on.

Review what has or hasn't worked in the past but don't dwell on the past or allow yourself to feel upset about the past. Being upset about what has happened in the past is one way of becoming trapped in the past and not living in the present.

We have not learned to time travel yet, so we can't change anything from our past. Therefore, if I am upset about a past event I will remain upset forever if I believe the only solution is for the event to have occurred differently. This does not mean that you should not resolve or make amends for past actions or words. There is nothing wrong with that and it is one way of resolving feelings about the past. Make amends if necessary.

Once you go through this process of letting go of the past to live more in the present you will reach a tipping point. You will find yourself reviewing the past less and less often and living more in the present. But there are several more things to understand before you can tip the scales dramatically and tune in fully to your Inner Guide's broadcast on "Present Radio", rather than personal judgment radio based on the frequencies of the past.

Keep in mind that personal judgment is at the opposite end of the continuum from Inner Guidance. As I wrote earlier we have years of intermittent reinforcement of the idea that personal judgment based on the past is the best way to find peace. The more strongly rooted in our personal judgment from the past as the guide to living a peaceful life the more distant we are from receiving Inner Guidance.

Fear and guilt in the subconscious mind block Inner Guidance

You might question the assertion from earlier that most people are spending 90% of their thinking in the past. You may feel that you don't spend much time at all thinking about the past. On the surface this is how it appears. We periodically think about the past but certainly not 90% of the time.

I will walk you through a little mind exercise to help elucidate this idea.

Take a moment to picture in your mind a favorite elementary school teacher. Hopefully you have one. If not, think of someone else from your childhood that you have not seen in a long time that brings up a warm fuzzy feeling for you.

Do you have a visual image of the person?

Is it a man?

A woman?

A Teacher?

A family friend?

A relative?

You may even be able to visualize the place where you saw this person the most often, a classroom, house or a part of the country.

The difference between what seems to be our moment by moment experience, "I don't think that much about the past", and my assertion that you are thinking about it 90% of the time or more is explained by the subconscious mind.

Have you ever heard a song for the first time in years and it instantly brings up your experience of life when you used to hear it regularly?

There is a perfume out there. I don't know what it is, but whenever I smell it, it brings back memories of a college girlfriend that wore that same perfume. I can be walking down a busy street and pass someone wearing that perfume and memories of that girlfriend and that time of my life pop up instantly.

Hopefully you were able to come up with a person from your childhood that you have a warm, fuzzy feeling about. As you read on, keep in mind how easily the thought of that person came to you once you were prompted by my question.

Before these prompts (my question about a person from your childhood, a song, or a perfume) occurred, where were these thoughts/memories? They are in your subconscious mind. These thoughts and memories are not floating around in the air and you reach out and grab them. You have them stored away in your subconscious. This should help you to realize that you have an entire lifetime of memories stored away. They are just not all conscious all of the time.

You have probably heard of, or personally experienced being in some frightening situation and not remembering the event. A commonplace example of this is a car accident. People often don't consciously remember the accident or the few minutes right before the accident. There are also those personal experiences such as physical or sexual abuse in which the victims and sometimes the perpetrators don't consciously remember the events. Keep in mind that some events that on the surface do not look all that traumatic can also get stored away and forgotten because of the level of fear they induce.

These are all examples of thoughts, memories, experiences which are in your subconscious mind. They are held there until they are brought into conscious awareness. This means that you have all of these thoughts and they are in your mind at all times just not all in your conscious mind.

My personal experience with this revolves around myself and my two older brothers John and Jeff. When I was 5, John 9 and Jeff 13, I witnessed Jeff beating up John. I don't remember what prompted the attack, but Jeff was dunking John's head into the bathtub and the toilet to the point where John was having trouble breathing. Witnessing this was scary for me as I was worried I would be the next victim.

Fast forward 20 years, I am 25, John 29 and Jeff 33. I am on vacation with my parents and John in California. Whatever discussion we are having prompts me to tell the story of John's near drowning at the hands of Jeff. John looks at me and says, "What have you been drinking. You must have dreamed that."

My parents assure me that the event never occurred.

I tell them, "Of course you don't know about this. Jeff threatened to kill John and I if we ever told you." Both my parents and John are united in their belief that this is an imagined happening.

I call Jeff back in Ohio and put him on the speaker phone so everyone can hear. I ask him if he remembers the incident of dunking John. He says he absolutely remembers and mentions a couple of facts about the incident.

John goes a little pale and looks very shocked. He can't believe this actually happened and that he does not remember it at all. Sometimes having a story like this retold prompts people to remember the incident. This was not the case for John. He still did not remember.

Since there is so much going on in the subconscious mind and much of it blocks access to our Inner Guidance it is important to take a look at it and understand how it operates.

90% of your thoughts are in your subconscious mind. For you math majors out there that means that 10% of your thoughts are conscious. This might still be hard to believe. Think of the examples above and how often you are prompted by something and a memory that you were not consciously aware of pops into your awareness. If you truly take a look at your thoughts from this perspective it becomes a little easier to accept that you are not consciously aware of most of your thoughts.

The subconscious mind is the reservoir for past memories, but it is not a physical location, it is a process. The subconscious is how the mind processes and deals with guilt and fear. This is why we can't remember some traumatic events that we have experienced. Physical or sexual abuse, car accidents, emotional abuse or neglect are all experiences that we process in our subconscious. The interesting thing about this is that you may even recall the traumatic event but not be aware of how you decided to deal with it, or what feelings you experienced at the time.

The subconscious mind gives us two tools to deal with our subconscious guilt and fear, projection and denial. In the earlier example of my brother John being physically abused by my brother Jeff we can identify some denial. John suppressed or denied the memory of that incident.

Projection is the mind's attempt to rid itself of some uncomfortable emotion. For instance, you feel angry that someone has called you a name and you blame or project the responsibility for your anger onto that person. "I am angry because Bobby called me a name." Or you feel angry that your parents divorced and you believe your life would be much happier if that had not happened. As you will find out in chapter 10, "My Feelings Just Landed on Me", you are completely responsible for your feelings and to blame someone else is projection.

It is hard to say how John projected that fear and guilt. One of the ways it could have showed up was as a fear of water. It is possible that John could have denied (forgotten) about the incident but projected his feelings about that experience into a fear of water. John may have gone through life being afraid of swimming, boating or even bathing without consciously understanding why. This would have been a great example of someone living in the past, with the past events dictating his current behavior. This did not happen for John but I guarantee he did project the fear and guilt he felt from that experience in some way.

Since my brother's experience has not provided us with a concrete example of projection it would be helpful to hear about someone that had an experience in the past dictate their behavior in the present.

In our Out of the Matrix trainings we often ask people to raise their hand if they can identify some behaviors that they participate in and they can't understand why. The entire room full of people inevitably raises their hands. I would imagine that if I asked all the readers of this book the same question, 99% could identify a behavior of theirs for which they can't understand their motivation.

When we have a repetitive behavior and we can't understand why we continue that behavior it is because it is being driven by a thought in our subconscious mind. Because so much of our thinking is subconscious we all have many behaviors for which the motivation is not obvious. We had a woman in one of our Out of the Matrix workshops describe the following story and subsequent denial and projection.

Kim was in her early 50's when she took the Out of the Matrix weekend workshop. At the age of 17 she had gotten into a car accident while driving with two friends. The car had slide down a steep embankment and flipped over. An ambulance arrived sometime after the accident and found Kim dragging the second of her unconscious friends up the embankment to the side of the road.

The EMT's from the ambulance sat Kim down, treated her wounds and tended to her two friends. Everyone was okay. Kim remembered getting into the car when their drive began and the next thing she could recall was being in the emergency room talking to a doctor several hours after the accident. She had no memory of the accident or of dragging her friends up to the side of the road.

The experience was so traumatic that Kim's mind suppressed the memory of it. She had no head or brain trauma that would explain her lack of memory. Having taken Out of the Matrix some 30 years after her car accident it was not an event she had thought much about in recent years.

In Out of the Matrix we spend time describing the subconscious mind and how it works. Kim shared her story of not remembering the accident or dragging her friends to safety. Her intent in sharing the story was so that people could have a real life example of a suppressed (denied) memory.

Several weeks after the workshop Kim was talking to her sister and the story of the car accident came up. Her sister asked, "Is that why you always freak out when there are car chases or accidents in movies?" Kim was stunned. She had never made the connection. Her sister was right. Kim couldn't stand movies that had car chases or crashes and would usually get very agitated and leave the theater or turn off the TV when a scene included these types of events. She realized that her experience of the car accident, which she did not consciously remember, was the cause of her behavior.

This is a classic example of projection. Kim was projecting the fear and guilt she felt about that accident onto her experiences with movies and television car chases and crashes. She blamed the movies for her feelings, not realizing it was triggering some upsetting thoughts in her subconscious mind.

We all have guilt and fear in our subconscious mind and because it is **Sub** –conscious (below, or out of conscious awareness) we deny and project it. This means that we often choose to behave in certain ways or have certain thoughts and the choice is driven by an experience and subsequent thoughts we are not aware of.

When I was a student teacher, there was a teacher in another program named Marge that felt the need to compare her students with those of other teachers. She was making the point that she thought her students were more difficult to deal with than anyone else's. I overheard her discuss this with a third staff member. Although I wasn't involved in the conversation I realized that Marge was revealing some subconscious thinking.

Her argument was clearly revolving around the idea that she had the tougher situation with her students. She wanted recognition/credit/kudos for her efforts with what she deemed as a more difficult student population.

I am going to read a few things into this situation. I believe that Marge had a subconscious rationale for her students to continue to fail. If she prided herself on how difficult her students were, she had a subconscious vested interest in them continuing to be difficult.

If I am correct in my interpretation of this situation, Marge would be making subconscious decisions that would keep her students struggling.

I did not work with Marge on a daily basis so I was not privy to her interactions with her students. But at one point one of her students was offered a job by another teacher. Several co-workers that were familiar with the job and the student felt that it would be a good first job situation for this young lady.

Marge was approached about the student getting her first paid job. Marge quickly rejected the idea on the grounds that she had unpaid positions at her vocational site that would be unfilled if her student took a paying job.

In the vocational special education field paid jobs are like gold. It is what vocational training is all about. Getting students into real life paid positions allows them to experience some degree of the adult world they will soon be entering, with school staff members supporting them and helping them to be successful.

I was shocked that Marge was rejecting this opportunity for her student. I checked in with several staff members that were familiar with the situation and they were similarly dumbfounded. I believe this was a manifestation of Marge's subconscious thought that her primary value as a teacher came from working with struggling students. If someone else provided a successful outcome for her students what would that say about her value as a teacher.

My understanding of Marge's motivation, that it was driven by subconscious thinking, is in part because there seems to be no rational explanation. Marge's argument certainly did not make sense. Whenever I hear someone trying to justify a self defeating behavior and their explanation makes no rational sense I know that they are acting from their subconscious thinking. In Marge's case it may not look like a self-defeating decision except that she is a vocational teacher with a goal of getting students paid jobs.

Interestingly, anytime you can look back on some behavior of **yours** and you are not sure why you chose to act the way you did, it is probably because there is something in your subconscious mind that is driving your behavior. This is especially true if the behavior is repetitive and self defeating. "Why do I keep choosing the same lousy Men to date?" or "Why do I continuously over eat even though I know it is unhealthy?" These are classic behaviors that are being caused by a subconscious thought. I say they are being caused by a subconscious thought because of the acknowledgment that I can't consciously identify the reason for my behavior.

My brother Jeff's addiction and story about the switch from cars to a moped is a classic example of denial and projection. Jeff was in denial about his drug and alcohol addiction. He did not consciously acknowledge that he had a problem. He then projected the cause of his struggles away from himself and onto cars. "I don't have a problem with drugs and alcohol, cars are the problem."

Jeff would later acknowledge that he knew all along that he had a problem with drugs and alcohol. But he never let that thought bubble up completely to the conscious surface of his mind. He avoided the thought, "I have a problem with drugs and alcohol" because it was too painful. In chapter 17, "Pain as the Gateway to Peace", you will read more about how important it is to look at your painful thoughts in order to release them.

"I eat compulsively", "I continually choose inappropriate partners", "I am always late", "I get drunk all the time." The first step in overcoming these seemingly out of control situations is to consciously acknowledge that it is happening. We can't affect a process if we are not consciously acknowledging that it is happening.

The classic example of this is the alcoholic. In Alcoholics Anonymous the first thing a recently sober individual is asked to do is acknowledge their problem, "Hi, my name is Bob and I am an alcoholic." With that in mind let's continue to understand more about how the Subconscious mind works and more specifically how it affects our behavior.

Hopefully all of this information has helped address my assertion at the beginning of this section that the vast majority of our thinking is about the past. Much of it is subconscious, but it is still **our** thinking.

We have established that the subconscious mind processes guilt and fear. Projection and denial are the two tools we are given to deal with the guilt and fear in our subconscious mind. Unfortunately, denial and projection do not help us reduce the level of guilt and fear in our subconscious. Projection and denial actually serve to anchor and expand guilt and fear in our minds.

Remember we want to reduce this guilt and fear because a reduction in guilt and fear will lead to an increase in peace and happiness. The greater our level of peace and happiness, the greater our connection will be with our Inner Guide.

In the second paragraph of this chapter I asserted that most people use the past as a guide for their decisions in the present moment and about the future. On the surface this looks like an appropriate way to handle things. And for many practical situations it is appropriate.

For instance I learn that the stove is hot (memory from the past) so I choose not to touch it now or in the future (decision in the present moment). Beyond these obvious practical situations, decisions made via Inner Guidance rather than the past produce a much more peaceful life.

Your probably wondering, "How do projection and denial serve to anchor and expand the guilt and fear we have in our subconscious?" Another excellent question!!

In order to understand the answer to this question we must first understand more about the guilt and fear that we are projecting and denying. As well as get an understanding of human emotions. Keep this question about projection and denial in mind as we cover these next two chapters on emotions.

Toolbox of ideas for Inner Guidance

1. Inner guidance trumps any other guidance.

2. Learning the language of Inner Guidance takes practice like learning a foreign language. Your Inner Guide is pure.

3. Your Inner Guide is **ALWAYS** broadcasting its message of peace. You need only to tune in.

4. Patience, less judgment and acceptance are mindsets that help you to match the frequency of your Inner Guide.

5. Pay attention to what thoughts bring you closer to Inner Guidance and repeat them as often as possible.

6. You must unlearn the language of judgment and learn the language of acceptance.

7. Your Inner Guide is the best judge of what is good for you!!

8. Acknowledging that you "Don't Know" what is best for you, opens you up to your Inner Guidance that does "Know" what is best for you.

9. You are tuned into the past because your thinking is mostly subconscious and the subconscious is filled with thoughts from the past.

Part 3

CHOICE AS A KEY TO
INNER GUIDANCE

Chapter 10
MY FEELINGS JUST LANDED ON ME

Fortunately feelings do not fly around and land on people. They also do not travel from other people like a ship floating on the ocean of their words and dock on us. Nor do feelings emanate from events and enter our bodies. Last but not least feelings do not exist in objects and when we see or interact with that object the feelings pass into our bodies.

Most people experience their feelings as just happening TO them and they have little control over them. One might say, "Every time I spend time with or think about my mother I feel angry, so it is clear to me that she is the cause of my anger." Therefore my mother needs to change if I am to not be angry around her.

This may be how someone experiences their mother. On the surface it looks like Mom makes me angry, she caused my anger. But how does that work? Do the feelings travel on Mom's words, enter my body and I experience them. Clearly not! I don't have to be in Mom's presence or even be actively hearing her words to be upset.

Or possibly you just bought some new item (car, house, dishwasher, blouse, pants, Smart Phone, kitten, etcetera). You are very excited about this new purchase. It certainly seems as if the new item is causing you to feel "excited." But again how does that work? Do the feelings exist in the item itself and as I interact with it the feelings enter me. Clearly not! I know this in part because I don't have to see, touch or even be anywhere near this item to feel the excitement.

There is one other way that I know that people, events and things don't cause feelings or experiences. There are **no** people, events or things that all people experience (think and feel) the same way about. You may experience anger every time you are around (or think about) your mother, but your best friend thinks your mom is wonderful and experiences contentment when she is in the presence of or thinks about your mom. Whereas, your grandmother may experience sadness when she is around your mother. This is an indication that Mom is not the cause of the feelings.

You may be excited and feeling joy about your new car purchase. But your neighbor feels jealous every time he sees your new car. Does the car engender feelings of Joy or feelings of jealousy? Does your mom engender feelings of anger, contentment or sadness? It depends on your perception or how you think about the car and your mom. We could go on and on with examples of how each person has a unique experience of the people, events and things in their lives, but you get the idea.

Keep in mind that the vast majority of the world operates from the premise that their feelings are caused by factors outside of themselves. This lends itself to the belief that their emotions are out of their control. They seem to be out of their control because they can't control how the people, events and things in their lives interact with them, and people believe that those things are the cause of their feelings.

This helps with understanding why the belief that factors outside of me cause my feelings has lead to a very unhappy world. When I believe that I can't control my emotions because they are dependent on factors outside of me it is not a stretch for life (specifically my own life) itself to seem out of control.

This brings us to the big question. If people, events and things don't cause our feelings, where do our feelings come from? Turn the page to find out!!

Toolbox of ideas for Inner Guidance

1. Inner guidance trumps any other guidance.

2. Learning the language of Inner Guidance takes practice like learning a foreign language. Your Inner Guide is pure.

3. Your Inner Guide is **ALWAYS** broadcasting its message of peace. You need only to tune in.

4. Patience, less judgment and acceptance are mindsets that help you to match the frequency of your Inner Guide.

5. Pay attention to what thoughts bring you closer to Inner Guidance and repeat them as often as possible.

6. You must unlearn the language of judgment and learn the language of acceptance.

7. Your Inner Guide is the best judge of what is good for you!!

8. Acknowledging that you "Don't Know" what is best for you, opens you up to your Inner. Guidance that does "Know" what is best for you.

9. You are tuned into the past because your thinking is mostly subconscious and the subconscious is filled with thoughts from the past.

10. People, things and events do not cause our feelings.

Chapter 11
EMOTIONAL CONTROL

You control your emotions. Your emotions do not control you!

I tell my students and my own children all the time, "You control your emotions. Your emotions do not control you." The struggle people have with this idea as described in the previous chapter is that this seems counter intuitive. It seems as if I interact with things outside of me and my emotions occur due to these interactions.

Alright, so what's the alternative? If the above belief system leads to limited happiness at best and an out of control life at worst how can one make a different choice. The first step is recognizing that you *do* have a choice. You can choose to be happy or return to your happiness relatively quickly in most situations.

The second step is to understand feelings, where and how they are produced. This understanding helps me to perform the first step and make a choice.

Feelings are chemicals! They are produced in the Hypothalamus, which is an almond sized organ in the brain. The hypothalamus produces chemicals that match *every* emotional state we experience. It produces chemicals for anger, sadness, joy, lust, frustration, excitement, anticipation and the list goes on and on. These chemicals are released by the hypothalamus into the blood stream and every cell in the body has docking sites that these chemicals dock on. Our experience of emotions is a release of chemicals into our blood stream!

Well, that certainly takes the romance out of things!! No one can make you sad, angry, happy or lustful. Instead, you are having a certain set of thoughts that trigger an emotional reaction within you. This explains my assertion in the previous chapter that to blame something outside of you for your feelings is projection. The responsibility for our feelings lies within each of us. Feelings are caused by our thoughts.

This is actually great news. If your emotional state were actually dependent on factors outside of you, such as other people, events and/ or things your emotions would be completely out of your control. Instead it is the exact opposite. Your emotional state is being produced inside of you and is controlled by how you think. Fantastic, this means that you can shift your thoughts in order to have a more peaceful life. Nothing outside of you needs to change at all. Keep in mind our end goal here is to expand our awareness of our Inner Guidance through living a happier more peaceful life.

Now let's examine the mechanics of how this process works. If someone calls you, "stupid", you have thoughts about being called stupid. One of the thoughts might be, "It is not okay for this person to call me stupid. He is embarrassing me in front of all my coworkers. They will all think I am a push over if I don't do something. I better get angry and stand up for myself." This whole thought process takes a fraction of a second to happen. The signal that is sent to the hypothalamus is, "let's get angry." The hypothalamus obeys and produces the chemical for anger. Because this all happens in a nanosecond (one thousandth of a second) it seems as if being called stupid caused you to get angry.

Here is another scenario for the same incident. After being called, "Stupid" you could have the following thoughts. "I am unconcerned with this person's opinion of me. I am much more interested in remaining peaceful than engaging in a verbal argument. I am just going to walk away, ignore this guy and think about the lovely weather and how much I love my wife." This thought process triggers the hypothalamus to produce peacefulness or calmness. The hypothalamus obeys these instructions and releases the chemical that matches the emotional state of peace and calm.

This is a very simple example of how our thinking controls our emotional state of being. It is not what happens to us that causes our feelings. It is our thoughts about what happens to us that causes our feelings.

> One Day my student Emily stormed into my office angry and complaining about something another student, Wayne, said. Now, Emily doesn't like Wayne at all.
>
> I listened to Emily angrily describe Wayne's offense. I then discussed with Emily the fact that she is giving Wayne the power over her feelings. "This is a person you don't like and you are allowing his behavior to make you upset. Is that really how you want to handle things? Allowing someone you don't like to have control over how your feelings?
>
> Once Emily is given this perspective on things she starts to feel differently. I can see her body start to relax. She starts to tell the story of Wayne's offense again but is not able to feel as upset. I explain to her that once she realizes what is happening, and that the upset is her choice she is not even able to get as upset. She recognizes that it is her choice how she feels about this interaction with Wayne.

It has also been discovered that these emotional chemicals burn out in 90 seconds. Therefore, if we are having a feeling and it lasts more than 90 seconds we are having more thoughts that are prompting another release of chemicals. This is one way of monitoring your progress in controlling your emotions. If your upsetting feelings are lasting more than 90 seconds you know that you are continuing to have thoughts that are triggering the release of chemicals that are causing your feelings.

Joy, happiness, guilt, fear, anger and sadness, are just a few of the emotions we as humans produce on a moment by moment basis. In chapter 9 we learned how influential the subconscious mind is on our emotional state. Since our subconscious is filled with guilt and fear it is helpful to understand the mechanics of guilt and fear. By understanding where our emotions come from we are much more capable of lowering the amount of guilt and fear that we end up storing in the subconscious mind. Especially since our goal is to feel more peaceful in order to connect with our Inner Guide.

The average person believes their emotions control them. In other words a person experiences an emotion and believes they are at the mercy of that emotion. When it runs its course, it runs its course and I am released from its impact. Most folks just wait until the event that seemed to trigger the emotion fades into the background. "I no longer consciously think about the event as much, so I no longer consciously feel the emotion."

But remember, the event is still in your mind, it is just not always a conscious thought. If you go to a party and someone mentions that event you will again be prompted to consciously think about it and you will have the same feelings as before.

Tony Senf and I were presenting the precursor to our Out of the Matrix workshop to some of my students. We had been meeting with my students for several months. My student Paul came in one day and shared the following story with us. This story is a beautiful example of someone taking a subconscious process and making it conscious.

"I was waiting for my girlfriend to pick me up last night. She was late and I hadn't heard from her. I noticed that I was starting to get very agitated. By the time she was 20 minutes late I was in a rage. But I started to wonder, "Why am I getting so upset." I recognized that my feelings about the situation were much stronger than the situation merited. People are late all the time.

So I began to think about why I was having such a strong reaction. It occurred to me that this upset was not about my girlfriend. It was about my mother. I always considered myself an abandoned person. My mom left my family and I when I was just 3 years old. I recognized that my girlfriend being late was pushing the buttons I have about my mom "abandoning" me when I was 3.

Once I recognized that my feelings weren't really about my girlfriend I started to calm down. In fact, in pretty quick order I was no longer upset at all."

Tony and I were blown away by the awareness that this young man had come to. Much of what he became aware of we had not discussed. Tony and I had to go over with him exactly what he had done. He had taken a subconscious process, "I am an abandoned individual and so I react to outside stimuli as an abandoned person would react." As an "Abandoned" person I view people's behavior towards me as either reinforcing my identity as "Abandoned" or negating it. When they are late I see this as validation that they don't care about me, and will therefore at some time leave me.

He had probably gone through this process hundreds of times before, with countless people. As his teacher I had certainly experienced reactions from him that were clearly triggered by his identification as "Abandoned." But on this occasion he brought it into his conscious awareness and was able to shift his experience (thoughts and feelings) about the situation.

For most people getting upset is a subconscious experience. In other words there is some thought in their subconscious mind that is prompting their upset. The upset takes over and they give very little thought to why they are upset. They believe that it is the event that is happening right in front of them that has caused their upset. Frequently though, perhaps 90% of the time, their feelings are being driven by some past experience.

There is one idea that I will express again here that helps me understand and believe in the idea that I control my emotional state of being. It is the idea that I can identify nothing that all humans experience in the same way. In other words every 15 year old who has their girlfriend or boyfriend show up late to pick them up does not react the same way.

I could run through a litany of people, things and events and people's varied reactions to these experiences. But the fact of the matter is there is nothing that all humans react to the same way. Reactions vary from person to person. This is because the reactions come from the person having the experience not the event, person or thing one is interacting with.

This is a very important distinction. You dictate how you feel by how you think. By thinking differently you can have a different thought/feeling/experience. This allows you to control your feelings.

It is time to answer our question from earlier, "How does projection and denial serve to anchor and expand guilt and fear in our subconscious mind?"

As you now understand it, you have produced every feeling you have ever had. To blame someone else for your feelings is a misrepresentation of power. You have the power to control your emotional state. This is why when we hold factors outside of ourselves responsible for how we feel we experience some level of powerlessness. Remember, if your feelings were caused by factors outside of you, factors which you have limited control over then you would experience very little control of your emotions.

You can understand now, why the belief that outside factors control my emotions would lead to the experience of powerlessness. The experience of powerlessness leads to the feeling of guilt because of your perceived inability to control your emotions. On some level you understand that your feelings are YOUR feelings and when you cede control of them to something other than yourself you feel guilty.

Trying to control how other people interact with us and/or control events in order to keep our emotions in line is like trying to keep your sidewalk clear of snow by catching each snowflake before it hits the ground. Both of these are impossible tasks and the belief that they are reasonable goals and therefore attempting to accomplish them, leaves us feeling frustrated and guilty.

You can certainly understand how trying to catch each snowflake before it hits the ground would be frustrating, but why would you feel guilty. You may recognize that catching each snowflake is impossible so you don't feel guilty about not being able to accomplish it. But most people really do spend much of their time and energy trying to manage the people and events outside of themselves in order to feel happy. When you really look at this concept you realize the magnitude of the difficulty. There is no way one can control the events and people in their lives. It really is like trying to catch those snowflakes. The difference is that we think it is possible to control outside factors in order to be happy. So when we can't accomplish this task we end up feeling guilty about our lack of Efficacy.

Now contrast that with you taking responsibility for your feelings. Once you begin to recognize that you can dictate how you feel by how you think your world changes dramatically. You are no longer at the mercy of other people or your current circumstances with regard to your feelings. You are empowered rather than powerless. Now, instead of trying to catch every snowflake, **you control the weather!!**

When we are blaming outside factors for our feelings we are projecting the responsibility for those feelings outside of us. This is why projection only serves to anchor and expand guilt in the subconscious. To reiterate an earlier point, when you are blaming factors outside of you for your feelings you will spend much energy trying to control those factors. Because you are unable to control factors outside of you, you will be left feeling powerless and guilty over your lack of Efficacy. Whatever feelings we are having they can't be shifted until their true origins, our thinking, are addressed.

Denial works similarly. Denying responsibility for something by denying that it happened or denying that I am responsible for it does not serve to resolve the situation. Denying that I am responsible for my feelings does not help me shift my feelings. It leaves me looking for a solution where there is none. This is an incredibly unreliable system for getting happy because you can't control outside circumstances.

Contrast that with relying on your thinking for your happiness. You are in control of your thoughts. Therefore you can choose how you think about everything and choose happy thoughts. This is a much more reliable system for feeling happy because you are relying on something you can control, your thinking, rather than something you can't control, events and people outside of you.

Along the lines of controlling your emotional state an Out of the Matrix workshop participant named Kimberly had a profound shift in her emotional state of being after taking the workshop. She called me a week after taking the weekend workshop and asked the following question.

"Chris, I know you are not a doctor but could it be possible that someone could take the Out of the Matrix weekend and have a significant enough shift that they no longer need to take anti-depressants?"

Now Kimberly was exactly right, I am not a doctor, nor do I play one on TV. So I was a bit hesitant to answer her question without some more information. I asked, "Why are you asking this question?"

Kimberly went on to explain that she had been on anti-depressants for 15 years since she was a teenager and had been suicidal. She explained that she tried to get off of her meds on numerous occasions but that whenever she got off of them she was "climbing the walls" with anxiety.

In the middle of the Out of the Matrix weekend she stopped taking her anti-depressants again and by the time she called she had not taken any in 8 days. She was feeling terrific and credited the explanation of how emotions work that she received in the Out of the Matrix workshop. She understood for the first time that her thinking was causing her depression and she could simply choose to think differently. My response was that she was an adult and that if she felt fine without her meds she should consult with her doctor and make sure there were no complicating factors. If according to her doctor there were no complicating factors then give life without meds a try. If the anxiety or depression returned she could always get back on the medication.

At the time of this writing, some 6 years later Kimberly is still medication free and she has become a facilitator for our Out of the Matrix program.

I am certainly not positing the idea that if you take Out of the Matrix you will no longer need to take medication. This story is presented here as a possibility. When you recognize what is actually happening and the level of control you have over your emotional state of being the possibilities of peace and happiness for your life are unlimited.

At an Out of the Matrix presentation a participant asked the following question: "Are you telling me that if my brother died tomorrow I shouldn't be upset about it?"

I understood the question. He was really saying, "You are telling us to choose peaceful happy thoughts all the time. That sounds unrealistic and here is an example of when I think that is an unrealistic task."

My answer to this query was: "No, I am not telling you how you should react to your brother's death. In fact I expect that you will be sad about it. And for my part, if my wife or children died tomorrow I would be very sad.

But I want you to understand that even the experience of death varies from person to person. One person might be devastated and go into a year long depression with thoughts of suicide because of the death of a loved one. Someone else would be sad and spend a month writing letters to the person that died in order to feel connected to them. After thirty days they have a greater sense of peace about the death, while still experiencing some sadness.

In the end I want you to understand that even our reactions to death are caused by how we think about the death, not by the death itself. But, I get that most people will experience sadness with regards to a death and that is perfectly fine. And in fact I know that all of us, including me, will have moments when we are not feeling happy. I just want you to recognize that on some level (usually subconscious) we are always making a choice to feel what we are feeling."

My life experience has been the most powerful reinforcement tool for my believing that I choose my feelings. I have spent years paying attention to my thinking and shifting to happier thoughts. I can unequivocally report to you that I am in control of my emotions. My emotions do not control me.

This does not mean that I don't get upset. But through this practice the following has happened for me. My upsets are much shorter in length, they are less intense, they happen less often and many things that used to upset me no longer do. You can understand how that would lead to a happier more peaceful life and in the process bring me into closer alignment with the frequency of my Inner Guide.

The preceding paragraph also speaks to the idea that there is an unlimited amount of happiness available to each of us. Again, my personal experience is that in using the techniques described in Living the Guided Life my life keeps getting happier and happier. At this point I see no end, no limit to this process. If I reach a limit at some point I will be sure to let you know.

Let's look at this from a cause and effect perspective. I understand that my thinking is the cause of my feelings. Therefore I spend time in the practice of paying attention to my thinking. When I catch myself having thoughts that lead to upsetting feelings I shift to different happier thoughts. Again I know this works because I have practiced it and I have all the evidence I need, in that, my life has continuously gotten happier, more peaceful and more guided.

I also have the alternative life experience. I spent the first part of my life believing that people, events and things caused my feelings. While living that belief system I spent tremendous amounts of energy trying to control people and events. I can unequivocally tell you that this belief system leads to a more and more sad, upsetting and disappointing life. I am eternally grateful that I have the two contrasting experiences. They allow me to recognize the futility of the one belief system and the beauty of the other.

I would encourage you to *not* believe in what I am explaining to you. Go out and try it and see if it works. That is the ultimate test. When the door to door vacuum cleaner salesman shows up at your door he doesn't just tell you how good his product is, he demonstrates it. He spills dirt on your carpet and vacuums it up before your very eyes. I am telling you about these techniques for living a happier more guided life. Now go out and practice them and see if they work. Don't take my word for it.

At the end of the section on the subconscious mind I asserted that projection and denial serve to anchor guilt and fear in our subconscious mind. Once again I tell you that this occurs because the responsibility for our feelings belongs with us. When we blame others we are attempting to make them responsible for our feelings. This projection of our responsibility for our feelings onto another does not lead to a lasting peace.

We attempt this process of projection over and over and over and over again. When it continuously does not lead to a lasting sense of peace we wonder, "What is wrong with me?" This question is usually asked subconsciously and inevitably leads to feelings of guilt over our inability to affect our own peace of mind. Our lack of understanding of how this process works causes us to store more guilt about our lack of Efficacy in our subconscious mind.

As this explanation points out, one of the keys to emptying our subconscious mind of guilt is recognizing our responsibility for our feelings. As you take responsibility for your feelings and reduce the amount of guilt in your subconscious your level of peace will grow leading to greater awareness of your Inner Guidance.

These last two chapters focusing on your feelings were designed to help you understand how projection and denial help to fill your subconscious with guilt and fear. If you desire to live a more peaceful and guided life you must stop denying your responsibility for your feelings and stop projecting that responsibility outside of yourself.

Toolbox of ideas for Inner Guidance

1. Inner guidance trumps any other guidance.

2. Learning the language of Inner Guidance takes practice like learning a foreign language. Your Inner Guide is pure.

3. Your Inner Guide is **ALWAYS** broadcasting its message of peace. You need only to tune in.

4. Patience, less judgment and acceptance are mindsets that help you to match the frequency of your Inner Guide.

5. Pay attention to what thoughts bring you closer to Inner Guidance and repeat them as often as possible.

6. You must unlearn the language of judgment and learn the language of acceptance.

7. Your Inner Guide is the best judge of what is good for you!!

8. Acknowledging that you "Don't Know" what is best for you, opens you up to your Inner. Guidance that does "Know" what is best for you.

9. You are tuned into the past because your thinking is mostly subconscious and the subconscious is filled with thoughts from the past.

10. People, things and events do not cause our feelings.

11. Your emotions are caused by **YOUR** thinking!

Chapter 12
INNER DIRECTED OR
OUTER DIRECTED

I t is time to label a few of the ideas that have been presented to make transference of this information easier.

One of the major obstacles to tapping into your Inner Guidance is the worldwide phenomenon of being "Outer Directed." This is a belief system that pervades our world. It is the belief that other people, things outside of us and our day to day circumstances dictate our feelings.

On the surface this looks like a credible belief system. "When I hear my mother's voice I start feeling angry." "When my team loses I feel sad." "When I get cut off in traffic I feel frustrated." "When my child gets in trouble at school I feel powerless." The list goes go on and on. It seems as if all these circumstances are the cause of the subsequent feelings. I hear my mother's voice and I feel angry. What other explanation is there for my anger than to hold my mom responsible for it. Sound familiar? You understand this differently now that you understand the biology of emotions.

Now we have a label for this type of thinking, "Outer Directed." "Outer Directed" is the belief system that maintains that my happiness and upsets are dictated by what happens outside of me.

I certainly have no problem with people living an Outer Directed life. The difficulty for the Outer Directed individual is he is dependent on the circumstances or other person changing for him to get back to his peace of mind. And we have already discussed how important it is to be in a peaceful state of mind in order to connect with your Inner Guidance.

Take a moment right now and think about the people, things and circumstances you encounter in your day. Put a percentage on how often these elements in your day meet your expectations. The day is sunny, 72 degrees, no humidity, your favorite breakfast is waiting for you, your car is full of gas, a coworker buys you lunch and your partner has prepared your favorite meal for dinner. Oh yeah, and everyone you meet during your day is pleasant, respectful and helpful.

You might experience a few of these things on a particular day but certainly nowhere near all of these things on a daily basis. If you have a day where all of this and more lines up for you make sure you buy a lottery ticket!

Let me be clear here, I am speaking of the days events lining up in a way that meets your preconceived expectations. I am not referencing the experience of seeing your day as perfect no matter what happens.

Of course you and I know that this Outer Directed stuff is pure bunk. We know this because we are aware that our feelings are produced by our hypothalamus that is prompted by our thoughts. You need only change your thinking about something and have different feelings on one occasion and you will have experienced the idea that you are in control of your feelings.

The fact of the matter is that everyone has been causing their feelings with their thoughts all along. Most folks are just not doing it consciously.

Since we are in charge of our own thinking we are responsible for our feelings. This belief system is called being "Inner Directed". "I believe that I am responsible for my thoughts and feelings, my happiness and upsets."

This is a "rubber meets the road" opportunity. Don't just believe what I am writing. Go out and try it. I have personally reduced my upsetting feelings exponentially by using this technique. See if you can think about something differently and not be as upset about it. Again if you have been alive for more than 5 minutes you have already done this, but now you will do it consciously. With the awareness of what is really going on.

I enjoy organized sports. In my younger days I was an avid follower of the professional sports teams in my hometown of Cleveland, Ohio. The Cleveland Browns are the local football team and I would allow the Browns performance on Sundays to dictate my week. If the Browns won I was in a good mood all week. If they lost I was miserable.

At some point I recognized the futility of this belief system. Allowing the outcome of a football game (that I had no control over) to dictate my mood for an entire week. One day I decided to handle the whole situation differently. I would allow myself to be upset about a Browns loss for 5 minutes after the game and then I would move on. I had made a decision to think and feel differently about the situation.

It worked beautifully. The Browns no longer dictated my mood during the football season. Thank goodness because the Browns have lost a lot more than they have won over the last 30 years.

My story of how I experienced the Browns is a perfect example of going from Outer Directed to Inner Directed. I recognized that I dictate how I feel based on how I think and I decided to think differently so I could feel differently.

It is as simple as that. Decide not to be upset about something and you will no longer be upset about it. Keep in mind that when you first start to practice this you will find it easier in some areas of your life than others.

Barb was an instructional assistant in our alternative high school for 2 years. She came to us with very little experience working with the defiant, angry, depressed and unmotivated student population that usually attended Alpha Tech.

Our instructional assistants would help to supervise our students in the Out of the Matrix classes. They would of course be exposed to the idea that they were responsible for their feelings.

Barb loved the Out of the Matrix classes and would frequently pick my brain about some of the ideas that it presented. One day she came to me because she was upset about the lack of respect she was encountering from the students. She found herself getting angry and wanting the students to treat her with more respect. Barb understood the idea that her feelings were being caused by her thinking but she found herself unable to shift her thinking so that she could be at peace. So she came to me wondering how to resolve this emotional situation.

I asked her why she thought the students were behaving disrespectfully towards her. After a brief discussion she understood that the students' disrespectful behavior was the projection of their lack of self-respect.

She came to this understanding as I pointed out how disrespectful the students were toward themselves. They took horrible care of themselves, both physically and emotionally. People who respect themselves respect others. Those that don't respect themselves don't respect others.

This was only half the story. We still needed to address her upsetting feelings. I went on to explain that it is flawed thinking to believe that respect from others is necessary. That is a very Outer Directed concept. Respect comes from inside of us.

Barb realized that the students' disrespectful behavior had nothing to do with her. There was no reason to be upset. It was simply a manifestation of how the students felt about themselves. Barb reported to me that from that point forward she no longer expected respect from the students. She knew she respected herself and did not need outside reinforcement. Funny thing was that the students began to treat her with more respect once she no longer desired it from them.

Barb's story is a great example of shifting from being Outer Directed to Inner Directed. She understood that she had some upsetting feelings. She understood they were coming from her thinking and she wanted to understand things differently so she would no longer be upset.

When you find yourself unable to shift your thinking about an event or a person so that you can be in peace, it is because the upset has actually tapped into some aspect of your negative self-image. In chapter 16, 17 and 18 I describe how to identify and release these negative self-beliefs so you can expand your connection with Inner Guidance.

Trust Facilitates Connectedness to your Inner Guide

Trust is one of the most important aspects of connecting with your Inner Guide. This means that you have to have some level of belief that your Inner Guide will help when you earnestly ask for its assistance.

Problem is you can't trust your Inner Guide if you don't first trust yourself. Trusting yourself in this vein refers to taking personal responsibility for how you experience life. When you choose to be Inner Directed you can trust yourself to handle all situations peacefully or at the least you can trust yourself to return to your peace relatively quickly.

Now we ask, "How does this work? How does being Inner Directed facilitate connectedness with my Inner Guide?" Your Inner Guide recognizes your innate power. When we shift our perception from Outer Directed to Inner Directed we are recognizing our innate power rather than giving it away to forces outside of us, thereby aligning us more closely with our Inner Guide.

Although I have only dedicated a few paragraphs to this idea of the development of trust it is the most important aspect of the process of connecting with your Inner Guide. I have only briefly touched on it because the natural outgrowth of the process described in this book is the development of trust. You only need to follow the processes in this book and you will be on your way to shifting your perception of yourself to the powerful being that your Inner Guide recognizes you are.

Toolbox of ideas for Inner Guidance

1. Inner guidance trumps any other guidance.

2. Learning the language of Inner Guidance takes practice like learning a foreign language. Your Inner Guide is pure.

3. Your Inner Guide is **ALWAYS** broadcasting its message of peace. You need only to tune in.

4. Patience, less judgment and acceptance are mindsets that help you to match the frequency of your Inner Guide.

5. Pay attention to what thoughts bring you closer to Inner Guidance and repeat them as often as possible.

6. You must unlearn the language of judgment and learn the language of acceptance.

7. Your Inner Guide is the best judge of what is good for you!!

8. Acknowledging that you "Don't Know" what is best for you, opens you up to your Inner Guidance that does "Know" what is best for you.

9. You are tuned into the past because your thinking is mostly subconscious and the subconscious is filled with thoughts from the past.

10. People, things and events do not cause our feelings.

11. Your emotions are caused by **YOUR** thinking!

12. Being Inner Directed brings me closer to my Inner Guidance, being Outer Directed takes me farther from my Inner Guidance.

Chapter 13
INTELLECT OR INNER GUIDANCE

I had a student who found himself at odds with our academic instructor on a regular basis. His defiance and downright mean and nasty attitude towards our entire academic staff did not make sense on the surface of things. His stated goal was to get good grades and graduate from high school. The staff was clearly in his corner in this regard and offered him regular support to achieve these goals.

Despite staff members that were clearly supportive of Carl and his goals he treated them like they were the enemy. Constantly at odds with them, you would have thought that they were attempting to ruin his life based on how he reacted to them.

I would have him in my office to discuss his behavior and how it was counter-productive. I would tell him, "The staff here only has the goal of helping you succeed. Your defiance and anger is only making it harder for you to accomplish **your** goals." To no avail my discussions seemed to have little to no effect on Carl's choices.

It got to the point where Carl became so disrespectful towards staff that he got suspended. As a point of understanding I don't often resort to suspension as a consequence for misbehavior. More often than not

I want to hear from the students that they understand their responsibility in the matter including that they are responsible for their own upset (hypothalamus and all!!). We work to dole out consequences that are meaningful, thought provoking and relevant. Suspension does not generally fall into that category. But in this case it was decided that suspension was necessary.

Now I can be a slow learner at times. I began this book with the story of receiving guidance to help my student Brad. This series of events with Carl took place 3 years after my experience with Brad. So, you would think I would instantly go to asking for Inner Guidance in this matter. But, my intellect really, really, really, really wants to be in charge and I have to consciously choose to set it aside in order to receive guidance.

After weeks of working with Carl I finally realized I was not asking for or tuning into my Inner Guide to help resolve this situation. Yeah, that's right. It took me weeks of struggle before I turned to my Inner Guide. Sounds silly since I am the author of "Living the Guided Life".

This helps to illustrate to me how powerful is my urge to use my intellect to navigate life. Honestly, on the surface, our intellect looks like a powerful ally that has helped us in a multitude of ways. But, and this is a big BUT, our intellect is quite ineffectual in comparison to our Inner Guide. It is like comparing the strength of a blade of grass with that of a giant redwood tree.

Now the only way you can buy into that comparison is to work to receive Inner Guidance and you will notice the difference in the results. In other words I can't appeal to your intellect with facts about the power of your Inner Guide in order to convince you to set your intellect aside. You will have to experience Inner Guidance and you will instantly know the appeal of the Guided Life.

Now back to my student Carl. I was in my office finishing up a particularly fruitless and frustrating conversation with him when it finally dawned on me to ask my Inner Guide to direct the conversation (Duh!!).

Keep in mind that our conversation was lightweight heated, both of us projecting some frustration at one another. He was getting up to leave when my Inner Guide had me tell Carl that he was treating the staff at our school like the enemy, as if we are out to ruin him and make him a failure. I pointed out what his goals were and how the staff was trying to support him in achieving those goals. "We are not the bad guys Carl", I told him. I could instantly see a shift in Carl. His facial features changed and his body relaxed.

This was a reiteration of what we had discussed many times, but the words were chosen by my Inner Guide not my intellect. Our discussion continued for just a few more moments and Carl left my office.

From that point forward Carl's experience of the staff shifted. It was not overnight, but he began to realize that he was sabotaging himself. He would come into my office trying to understand his feelings so that he could shift them, rather than coming into my office complaining about the staff and wanting them to change.

Remember, I had spent weeks working with Carl on these issues. I racked my brain/intellect for what to say and how to say it to guide Carl to make a shift in order to help himself. I had had years of work with teens and my intellect had served me well. I had cause to believe I could figure it out based on my past successes. You can see that I was not getting to the "I Don't Know" mind. I was in the, "I am going to apply as much intellectual force to this situation as possible" mind.

Luckily my Inner Guide was working with me. It provided me with a case that my intellect would not be able to crack. My Inner Guide was providing me with yet another experience of recognizing its power vs. my intellectual force. I asked for guidance and three sentences later the entire situation changed. My intellect had been working on the problem for weeks to no avail.

The message that I was guided to give Carl was not that different from the message my intellect was providing. But, there was something about the way the guided message came across that resonated with Carl. My Inner Guide knew what Carl needed to hear.

This experience with Carl was a huge reminder for me that my intellect is incredibly limited in its awareness and ability to help me and others.

Toolbox of ideas for Inner Guidance

1. Inner guidance trumps any other guidance.

2. Learning the language of Inner Guidance takes practice like learning a foreign language. Your Inner Guide is pure.

3. Your Inner Guide is **ALWAYS** broadcasting its message of peace. You need only to tune in.

4. Patience, less judgment and acceptance are mindsets that help you to match the frequency of your Inner Guide.

5. Pay attention to what thoughts bring you closer to Inner Guidance and repeat them as often as possible.

6. You must unlearn the language of judgment and learn the language of acceptance.

7. Your Inner Guide is the best judge of what is good for you!!

8. Acknowledging that you "Don't Know" what is best for you, opens you up to your Inner Guidance that does "Know" what is best for you.

9. You are tuned into the past because your thinking is mostly subconscious and the subconscious is filled with thoughts from the past.

10. People, things and events do not cause our feelings.

11. Your emotions are caused by **YOUR** thinking!

12. Being Inner Directed brings me closer to my Inner Guidance, being Outer Directed takes me farther from my Inner Guidance.

13. I must let go of my intellect's desire to be in control if I am to tune into my Inner Guide's broadcast.

Chapter 14
BEHAVIOR CYCLES

In chapter 9 I wrote about the subconscious mind and that the primary tools we are given for dealing with the guilt and fear in our subconscious mind are projection and denial. In our efforts to live a happier more peaceful life in order to tap into our Inner Guidance it is important to understand the myriad ways we project guilt. This chapter describes one of the primary ideas humans believe in that facilitates the projection of guilt.

This primary idea that prevents us from tapping into our Inner Guidance is: "In order to stop an unwanted behavior a person should feel badly (guilty) about that behavior." I will refer to this "feeling bad" about a behavior as Emotional Punishment. As a point of understanding I am referring to how humans tend to think negatively about themselves when they have made a mistake. This is not exclusive to our own mistakes, we also believe that we should emotionally punish others for behaviors and thoughts they have engaged in and that this will stop them from engaging in this behavior or thinking.

Examples of this might include: Feeling bad about cheating on a diet when the reason you overeat in the first place is because you don't feel good about yourself. Another common example is a parent giving their child a mean/angry/dirty look when they are doing something the parent finds unacceptable. Think carefully about this parent, child scenario. When that nasty look occurs what is the thought process behind it. If you consider it honestly I think you will agree the motive is to make the child feel badly about what they are doing so that they will stop.

This is one of those counterintuitive moments. It certainly appears as if this technique works and is valuable. "I give my child a dirty look and they stop talking to their sibling during a church service." Why is this exchange anything but valuable and productive?

This exchange is not valuable because the purpose of the look is to make someone feel guilty. I am not coming from a place of peace. If I am not coming from a place of peace I am interrupting the flow of information from my Inner Guide.

As a parent I am attempting to elicit the feeling of guilt from my child. But from the perspective of Living the Guided Life this makes no sense. I certainly want to contribute to my child's connection to Inner Guidance and intentionally behaving in a way that is designed to elicit guilt from my child, moves me and my child away from Inner Guidance.

I want to be clear that I think it is completely acceptable to work to keep your child quiet during a Church service. I just believe there are ways to do this that are not designed to elicit guilt from the child in order to get him to stop.

If this universally applied idea that eliciting guilt from myself and others is not the way to change unwanted behavior then what is? How can I get myself to stop behaving in self destructive ways or in socially unacceptable ways and help others make a similar choice? It would be impossible for me to come up with an answer for all the potential scenarios that you might find yourself in, but I can tell you the answer is to check in with your Inner Guide. Your Inner Guide does have answers for any scenario that you find yourself in. I can guarantee that the Guidance you will receive will not be designed to elicit the feeling of guilt from anyone.

I recently had an assistant who was struggling with showing up to work on time. I was her direct supervisor and had several discussions with her about her arrival at work 5-10 minutes late almost every day. I wanted to help her understand that this behavior would damage her ability to move onto other positions and it affected our ability to run our program effectively.

After several discussions the tardiness got better for a little while but then she would fall back into the same habit. This individual was clearly distraught about her own behavior. It was not a conscious defiance of authority that was causing her to be late. Consciously she wanted good evaluations because she wanted to move on to a better paying job within our school district. She understood completely that she was sabotaging her own goals.

The real story here is about my internal struggle with the situation. I would be aware of my assistant's late arrival, and aware of my own belief that making people feel guilty about mistakes is not a valuable way to alter behavior. I would always greet her pleasantly and I would not mention the inconvenience that her late arrival caused. She was well aware of the inconvenience, as I had pointed it out in our private discussions.

Man Oh Man there was a part of my mind (ego) that was screaming at me, "You can't let her get away with this again, come down on her now." I would eschew this suggestion and return to the idea of teaching not punishing. Then my ego would back off and offer a less severe suggestion, "You have to at least give her a look of disapproval so that she knows you are upset." Again I eschewed this suggestion because this was still the projection of guilt, which I teach is not a valuable practice for human growth let alone for tapping into Guidance. The battle lines were drawn in my mind. Do I listen to my ego and "Nail" this person for their mistake or do I listen to my Inner Guidance. My Inner Guide was clear that I needed to meet with my assistant privately and help her understand her self-destructive behavior so she could make a conscious choice to change.

In our meetings it was clear that she was starting to understand the cause of this pattern of tardiness that extended to parts of her life outside work. Then one day she was 40 minutes late for work and I woke her up with my phone call. She had overslept!! When she came in I required an explanation for why she was now over an hour late for work. I must point out that throughout this process I maintained a supervisory role in that she received the poorest rating for punctuality on her evaluation and her tardiness affected several other categories on her evaluation. Although I know that she felt badly about these evaluations it was important that she get honest feedback about her performance on the job. The evaluations were not done to elicit feelings of guilt but simply to help this person understand that this behavior was going to affect her ability to achieve her goals.

A month later she overslept and was an hour late again. At this point I met with her and discussed going to the administration about her moving onto another program or classroom within our school or our school district. I felt that maybe a change in scenery would do her some good.

She was flabbergasted that I was going to "Dismiss" her from our school. She thought, correctly, that I and the other staff members liked her. In the rest of her life one of the ways she got around irresponsible behavior was by being very likable. "Being Liked" had been a kind of free pass.

At this point I had to explain that although I had no desire for her to feel badly about her behavior there is such a thing as natural consequences. If you can't do the job in the manner that is required then you lose the job. This was quite a shock to her system. "I am going to be held accountable for my behavior despite being liked?" This was not a direct quote but her comments pointed toward this mentality.

During this entire process I could hear my ego continue to implore me to project some guilt. I frequently found myself needing to set aside this mentality so that I could get Guidance.

In the end she asked for a second chance. I agreed to a second chance with a few stipulations, which are not important to detail here. The shock of being held accountable helped her to reboot and tardiness has not been an issue since.

The lesson in this story is twofold. One is to not react to our default mode of operating which is to project guilt onto those whom we deem are making mistakes. In this way we are maintaining a peaceful state of mind and therefore receiving Guidance.

Second is to hold people accountable for their behavior in a loving and positive manner. By doing this we are again maintaining our connection with Guidance and helping them to help themselves become successful.

I am able to maintain this mentality of peace by understanding that my role in such situations is "Teacher" not "Judge." This allows me to help people grow not punish them for wrongdoing.

I can't tell you how eye-opening the above story was for me. It really drove home for me that even with all the work I have done on having a peaceful mind my first instinct was to project guilt. I still need to overcome my first instinct in order to maintain my peace of mind and therefore my connection with Inner Guidance.

We Are Hardest on Ourselves

I believe that people who engage in self-destructive behaviors are doing so because they are in emotional pain. In the category of "Self-Destructive" I include behaviors that are directed towards others such as violence, cheating, lying, or even being late for work. I call these self-destructive because these behaviors cause people difficulties, they do not bring them peace. Therefore they are self-destructive even though they are directed towards others.

It is once again valuable to interject the idea of a continuum. The degree to which someone engages in a self-destructive behavior is directly related to how much emotional pain they are in. Someone who engages in a self-destructive behavior once a week is not in as much emotional pain as someone who engages in a self-destructive behavior 10 times a day.

Now, I know what you are thinking. The person who engages in the self-destructive behavior 10 times a day is feeling even more emotional pain by the end of each day. That is exactly right! This happens because we believe that feeling bad (emotional pain) about a behavior will cause us to stop engaging in the behavior. Problem is that I engaged in the behavior in the first place because I was in emotional pain. If I believe that inflicting emotional pain on me for a bad behavior is the way to stop the behavior, I feel worse after each time I engage in the behavior.

Let's take the story of my assistant from above and look at in the light of the last three paragraphs. It turns out that she was adopted by two alcoholic parents who had both gotten sober in the three years before she joined our program. As you can imagine being raised by two alcoholic parents left my assistant with some wicked emotional scars. Not the least of which was the belief that she was "incapable."

Here she was living up to the "incapable" belief by not being able to do the most basic aspect of a job - show up on time!! Coming from the alcoholic family background she felt badly about herself. Each and every time she was late she would feel worse about herself, but feeling badly about herself was the major cause of her tardiness in the first place. Making her feel worse about it was not going to help.

You can see the cycle of behavior that occurs in this instance. I am in emotional pain in part because I don't like a behavior I just participated in and I emotionally beat myself up for that behavior. Now I feel worse about myself, more emotional pain, which leads to more harmful behavior. Round and round the Behavior Cycle goes where it stops nobody knows!

I have a former student named Josh that had molested his younger stepsister and because of this was removed from his house and lived in a group home for a number of years.

Sexual abuse is rarely isolated. In other words, when someone perpetrates sexual abuse upon another, more often then not they were abused themselves in the past. This was the case with Josh. He had been sexually molested by a stepbrother on a regular basis from the ages of 5-10.

One day Josh was having a particularly hard time functioning at school. Not able to focus on work, pacing around the classroom and being somewhat nasty and defiant towards staff members. I asked Josh to step into my office to discuss his difficulties.

It turned out that the next day Josh would not be in school because he was to attend a meeting with his stepsister's therapist. Josh, his parents, his stepsister, her therapist and Josh's therapist would all be in attendance at this meeting. This was to be the first time Josh would see his stepsister since he had been removed from the house.

As if seeing his stepsister for the first time wasn't difficult enough, the meeting's purpose was to decide if Josh was ready to return to the family home. Having been removed from the home Josh had undergone intensive therapy to help him deal with what had happened to him and what he had done to his stepsister.

In everyone's eyes Josh had made tremendous progress. He understood why he made the decision to molest his stepsister, he had matured as an individual and he had healed some of his personal pain.

The therapists involved in Josh's case were experts in the field. They specialized in dealing with sexual abuse. I trusted that they would be able to discern if it would be safe for Josh to return to his home. Josh certainly still had many issues and was not a healed and happy person. But, again he had definitely made a lot of progress since being removed from the home. All this explained Josh's agitated state of mind.

Before I tell you about my exchange with Josh I need to let you know that I believe that removing Josh from his home was the correct decision. When someone is at risk of physical or psychological harm I absolutely believe that steps must be taken to protect people. I also believe that if people are a threat to others they should be removed from society until they can be rehabilitated to the point of safely returning.

In my office Josh shared with me his varied concerns about how the meeting the next day would turn out. As you can imagine he was concerned about his stepsister's reaction to him and about what conclusion would be drawn about his potential return to the family home. I was guided to offer a radical idea to Josh.

I told Josh that he should not feel badly about what he had done to his stepsister. That is not a misprint. I told Josh he should not feel bad about molesting his stepsister. Josh was flabbergasted at this statement. "What are you talking about, I molested my stepsister. Of course I should feel bad about it." he responded.

Josh had been through our Out of the Matrix training and the concepts in this chapter are covered in the Behavior Cycles section of the training. So he had heard the idea that feeling bad about a behavior only contributes to feeling bad, not healing. As well as the idea that feeling bad is the cause of self-destructive behavior in the first place.

I asked Josh how he was feeling about himself and life in general when he molested his stepsister. He got into some detail about the dread he carried with him on a daily basis at that point in his life and that he still had some of those feelings but had learned different ways to deal with them.

I asked Josh, "If I could reach into your mind and remove any emotional pain you have, would you ever molest anyone ever again?"

He had to think about this. He responded, "But you can't remove all my emotional pain."

"You are correct, but I ask that question to make a point. It is the emotional pain that caused you to engage in this self-destructive behavior. No, no one can remove your emotional pain, but there is no need to add more emotional pain. I certainly believe that you needed to be removed from the house and that you needed/need healing. You need to continue to earnestly work on understanding why you behaved the way you did, so that you will not make that choice again. You needed/still need to be rehabilitated, not emotionally punished."

I went on to explain that I was not suggesting that Josh should feel positive about the molestation. He needed to understand that it was a mistake. Mistakes require correction not punishment. In his case the correction needed to occur in his mind. Good therapy is designed to do just that, correct our thinking so that we do not continue to make the same mistakes. Intellectually Josh understood what I was explaining to him, in part because of what he had learned in Out of the Matrix. This concept of not inflicting emotional pain for perceived misbehaviors is a radical one for anyone to integrate into their life. I did not expect that Josh would be able to shift his perception of himself and the situation in that moment in my office. But, I understood that I was planting a seed, an idea that could grow in his mind over time. I went on to explain to Josh that in that meeting the following day the need for him to feel bad about what he did to his stepsister would probably come up.

I discouraged him from mentioning that I told him he should not feel badly about what had happened. Without the background from the beginning of this book, the Out of the Matrix training or some similar information folks would surely think I was off my rocker for suggesting he should not feel badly for molesting his stepsister.

I am not an expert on sexual abuse and would never put myself in a situation where I was to decide if someone in Josh's situation should return to his home. I trust that the therapists in this situation would be able to make that assessment.

The day after the meeting Josh informed me that they decided he was not ready to return home. On one level Josh was disappointed, but on another level he knew it was the correct decision. He was not ready to return home. Other than that the meeting with his stepsister went reasonably well.

The part of the meeting he was most interested in telling me about was the rationale that was presented for why he could not return home. His stepsister's therapist told Josh that he did not feel bad enough about what he had done and therefore was not ready to return. He said, "You were right. They think I should feel worse about what I did, and that doesn't make sense." My hope was that Josh would be able to use this experience as a template for future mistakes. "Don't beat yourself up for a mistake. Understand why it happened and correct the mistake." It is that simple.

It is strange, but on one level I agreed with the decision made at Josh's meeting. I did not believe he was ready to return home either. But, I would not have framed the reason for the decision around the idea that he did not feel badly enough about what had happened. My feeling was that Josh needed more time to understand himself, his motivations and his struggles. Through this increased awareness he would be able to make different choices.

Josh's story is an extreme example. But the same concepts hold true for all mistakes no matter how significant they are perceived to be. It seems counterintuitive to not emotionally beat yourself up for something like cheating on a diet. "What is wrong with me. I've been doing so well then I go and eat that huge piece of chocolate cake with Oreo crumbs and whipped cream all over it (anyone's mouth watering?) and ruin three days of calorie counting." This inner dialogue looks pretty harmless and maybe even looks helpful when looked at on the surface. Instead I need to understand what went wrong, why did I choose to eat a 1000 calorie desert when I know it goes against my well-being.

Of course we need to look at this through the lens of growing our connection with our Inner Guidance. Emotional pain is not a frequency your Inner Guide can broadcast on. Remember it broadcasts on the peace and love network. When you choose to understand your mistakes and correct them rather than inflicting emotional pain upon yourself you are much more likely to pick up on your Inner Guidance.

This is all fine and dandy as an internal concept. "I don't want to beat my self up for my mistakes any more." But, now we need to examine how this impacts our relationship with others. Yes, when we beat ourselves up we are moving away from the peaceful thinking that links us to our Inner Guide. When you judge someone else and think that they should suffer or feel emotional pain for what they have done you are again moving away from a peaceful mind.

I am sure you know of someone who harbors anger towards a parent. Maybe it's you. This occurs for some people long after their parents are dead.

Let's look at that philosophy in more depth. I harbor anger toward my parents' behavior that occurred years ago. To what end? What does this way of thinking do for me? Take a moment to really think about that. What does being angry at anyone really do for you, especially someone who is dead and gone?

My students have been a tremendous help to me in learning to validate all the points that I make in this book. Darrell was a 17 year old student of mine. He was particularly angry at his mother because she had beaten him earlier in his life, to the point where he was left with scars. For a time Darrell was removed from his mother's care because of these beatings.

His mother eventually received some help and when I met her she had turned a corner. Darrell had been returned to her care and she acknowledged the mistakes that she had made and she had become a caring, loving mother. Not a perfect parent, mind you (there is no such thing as a perfect parent) but a more caring and understanding parent.

Darrell was still walking around with the physical and emotional scars of his earlier childhood. As you can imagine Darrell had some anger issues. He would get into frequent fights and verbal tirades directed towards teachers and peers.

After a particularly nasty outburst at school I asked Darrell to join me in my office. He had calmed down so he and I began to talk about his behavior. Darrell had been through Out of the Matrix so he was familiar with many of the ideas In "Living the Guided Life." After some discussion I was guided to turn the conversation to Darrell's mother.

I asked, "Are you ready to forgive your mother?" To which Darrell replied with an adamant "No." I was guided to pursue this vein of the conversation further even though he and I had never talked about his relationship with his mother in any depth.

I asked him who all the anger he was holding towards his mother was impacting the most. There was a long pause. Darrell knew the answer. He realized that holding the anger and rage towards his mother was making his life much more difficult. He acknowledged this in the meeting with me.

I made the obvious point, if the anger you are harboring has the greatest impact on you, and it is as you have acknowledged, almost exclusively a negative impact, why don't you forgive your mom and let the anger go. Again, he understood the question but indicated that despite the negative impact on his life and knowing that his anger was having little to no affect on his mom he was not willing to forgive her and let go of his anger.

I totally understood where Darrell was coming from. Many of us have similar feelings about people who have harmed us or even harmed others. We believe that it will somehow serve me, the culprit, or society to harbor angry feelings.

Many people will acknowledge that harboring anger does not serve them. Yet, they continue to do it. Darrell, like most people, believed that forgiving his mom would be letting her off the hook. He wanted her to suffer at the hands of his anger. But, intellectually he understood that his mother had changed and acknowledged her mistakes and that his anger had little to no effect on her.

This story about Darrell and his mother is a great example of how people harbor the idea that emotional punishment will produce a beneficial result. Fortunately it does not work that way. But it is a very tough concept for people to give up.

I had a woman at a workshop ask me if it was okay for someone to feel a little bad about something they had done. She was having a hard time giving up the idea that feeling bad was not the answer. My reply was that people are very good at making **themselves** feel bad about their mistakes. There is no need for us to "Pile On" and work to make the individual feel worse about what they had done.

Anyone who is being honest with themselves will understand to what I am referring. **Everyone** is well versed and expertly capable of emotionally beating themselves up. This is in fact the default human response to mistakes. Instead work to correct the mistake. This often entails recognizing how thinking and/or behavior is sabotaging happiness/success.

As you read this chapter and consider the ideas it contains I think you will come to a conclusion similar to mine. That the idea of making people (including ourselves) feel bad about a behavior is not a viable method of encouraging personal growth. We must see ourselves as teachers, not punishers.

I know that the ideas in this book and more specifically in this chapter may be considered radical on some level. Universally speaking if you look at human history I believe you will see that the idea of emotional punishment as our primary tool for growth has always been a mainstay or societal norm. I believe that if we want things in our world to radically change to peace as the norm, we need to embrace some radically different ideas than those that have been around for thousands of years.

Toolbox of ideas for Inner Guidance

1. Inner guidance trumps any other guidance.

2. Learning the language of Inner Guidance takes practice like learning a foreign language. Your Inner Guide is pure.

3. Your Inner Guide is **ALWAYS** broadcasting its message of peace. You need only to tune in.

4. Patience, less judgment and acceptance are mindsets that help you to match the frequency of your Inner Guide.

5. Pay attention to what thoughts bring you closer to Inner Guidance and repeat them as often as possible.

6. You must unlearn the language of judgment and learn the language of acceptance.

7. Your Inner Guide is the best judge of what is good for you!!

8. Acknowledging that you "Don't Know" what is best for you, opens you up to your Inner Guidance that does "Know" what is best for you.

9. You are tuned into the past because your thinking is mostly subconscious and the subconscious is filled with thoughts from the past.

10. People, things and events do not cause our feelings.

11. Your feelings are caused by **YOUR** thinking.

12. Being Inner Directed brings me closer to my Inner Guidance, being Outer Directed takes me farther from my Inner Guidance.

13. I must let go of my intellect's desire to be in control if I am to tune into my Inner Guide's broadcast.

14. You must let go of your belief that inflicting emotional punishment is the best way to help people change behaviors/evolve, this is not a frequency that your Inner Guide broadcasts on.

Part 4
REDEFINING YOU TO CONNECT WITH INNER GUIDANCE

_____ *Chapter 15* _____
PERSONAL RESPONSIBILITY

Taking Your Guidance to the Next Level

Most of what I have written about to this point revolves around taking personal responsibility for your life. Taking personal responsibility for your life (consciously choosing your feelings) is one of the quickest and most efficient ways to then turn your life and its direction over to your Inner Guide. This begins with the idea that you are responsible for your feelings. How you think about things activates your hypothalamus to release chemicals that you experience as emotions. Awareness of this idea is the belief system we call being Inner Directed – "I am responsible for my happiness and my upsets."

The connection with your Inner Guidance does not necessarily open up once you recognize and accept that you are responsible for your feelings. You must take the next step and take advantage of the fact that you produce your emotional state with your thinking by consciously choosing your thoughts.

Once you have this belief system on board you can work to make your life happier and more peaceful each and every day. To this point I can report that there seems to be no end to this process. I still work to choose happier and more peaceful thoughts and my life just keeps getting happier, more peaceful and more guided.

As your connection with your Inner Guide expands you come to a new and different awareness. Yes, I am responsible for my life and how I interact with it. Yes, my awareness of my Inner Guidance has increased, thanks to living an inner directed life and therefore choosing more peaceful thoughts. In fact the more time I spend listening to my Inner Guide the more trust I build with it. I turn to it more and more often for answers to my daily struggles.

As I have paid attention to my relationship with my Inner Guide a few things have become apparent to me. The first thing is pretty obvious based on what I have been writing about: I can ask for answers or what to say or do. The second thing is that the answers that are presented to me seem to work beautifully and seamlessly. By seamlessly I mean that Guided answers work out without any kinks or any need on my part to tweak anything. In fact, I find that Guided answers require much less of me than my ego might like. Often the answers require nothing of me. Boy, does that drive my ego crazy.

As a teacher in an alternative high school I work with students that struggle with being successful in the typical high school. These struggles often show up as defiance of teachers and other authority figures. I had one such student that had such intense anxiety that he had trouble sitting still and tremendous difficulty focusing on anything, especially school work. He frequently got himself into trouble and required constant staff supervision. His regular complaint was that he did not want to have to stay in school all day.

In our staff meetings we would discuss this student and how we could help him become a more functional person. We often found ourselves at a loss as to what to do. I would coach him regularly (frequently checking in with my Inner Guide) on how to handle things and how he was sabotaging his own success. He definitely understood what I was explaining to him but there was very little change in his behavior.

To make a long story short I realized that this situation required a level of guidance beyond my asking for what to say or do. I asked my Inner Guide to solve the problem. "Take this problem and resolve it."

I must admit that as teacher of students with emotional and behavioral difficulties my ego feels like it is responsible for solving the issues that arise in our school and with my students. This thought leads to some resistance on my part to turning to something that is not my ego to solve a difficulty. But, with more and more practice at "turning things over", I have had less and less resistance.

On Thursday I went home after a particularly frustrating day with this student and turned to my Inner Guide for a resolution. I simply sat quietly and recognized that my intellectual process was not resolving the issue. I then asked my Inner Guide to resolve this situation. "Present a solution to me." I did this earnestly, with a belief that my Inner Guide **could** resolve the issues.

The greater my belief that my Inner Guide can resolve any issue will hasten the solution's appearance. This occurs in part because the more belief I have in my Inner Guide the less reliance I have on my intellect. By setting aside my intellect I am getting to the "I don't know mind." In the "I don't know" mind I will be able to recognize the Guided solution when it is presented.

One of the options my student and I had pursued was finding him a job so that he could be released from school early to work. This idea appealed to my student since it would lead to money in his pocket and less seat time at school. My intellect did not hold out much hope of getting a job for a 16 year old with no work experience and significant issues with focus and defiance.

On Friday this student was absent which was a relief to the staff because he was such a time consuming student. Monday morning he came in and reported that he had gotten hired at a local restaurant. They wanted him to work from 9am to 1pm daily. This presented a solution I would never have considered. I immediately knew what had happened. My Inner Guide provided a resolution.

We arranged that this student could submit his school work on Monday mornings, with 80% or better on all assignments, and he would be allowed to work instead of attending school on a daily basis.

On the surface, allowing a student with defiance and attention issues not to attend school regularly might not look like an ideal situation. As I spoke with the staff members from his home school and his father, everyone agreed to give this setup a chance. One reason for everyone's agreement was the fact that most other options had been exhausted and we might as well try an extreme option and see if it works.

This solution offered various benefits to all parties. School staff could stop beating their heads against the wall trying to get this round peg (student) to fit into a square hole (the school environment).

My student could stop expending massive amounts of energy trying to avoid school work and defy his teachers. It also provided a physical outlet for my student's anxiety as he liked to keep moving and this was a physical job.

The appearance of this option took very little if any effort on my part. A huge and beautiful lesson for me: If I allow my life to be directed by my Inner Guide and not by my ego things work out with little to no effort on my part.

I have used this method for resolving issues in our school so frequently that staff members who were unfamiliar with my alternative school methods have nicknamed our program, "The Do Nothing Program." I am clear that this moniker was developed because from outside the system it could appear at times as if things "**Flow**" very easily in our alternative school. It appears as if very little effort is being expended on the part of the staff.

Mind you, we have vastly positive outcomes with students who had come to our program because of failing grades, credit deficiencies and behavioral problems. Most of our students had been in several alternative schools with little to no success. We have students that the school system had run out of options for and we were being successful with. Yet we were being called the "Do nothing program."

Hopefully you are wondering about the capitalized and bolded **"Flow"** in the previous paragraph. Flow in this sense is a reference to working with your Inner Guidance. It is actually your more natural state to be connected constantly with your Inner Guide. To not listen to your Inner Guidance creates dissonance, resistance or lack of "Flow" in your life because you are going against your natural state of being.

When a system, like our school, is taking advantage of its Inner Guidance, life flows more easily because the individuals in the system are more closely aligned with their natural state of being. To use my ego to resolve situations creates resistance because it is going against my natural inclination towards Inner Guidance.

If you are unaware of any of the concepts presented in this book, you might look at a system that uses Inner Guidance and think that the system isn't doing much work even though the system has positive outcomes (like our school) on a regular basis.

In reality the system that uses Inner Guidance is doing very significant work. The people in that system are working to be Inner Directed. Although on the surface it might look like there is less happening, the Inner Directed individual is working to discipline his own mind, making distinct choices in how he perceives the world and is interacting with the world.

Let's go back to my snowflake analogy. Remember, being Outer Directed and trying to control multiple factors outside of myself in order to feel happy is like trying to catch every snowflake before it lands on my driveway. Being Outer Directed also leads to a much more scattered mind. I must constantly consider multiple factors outside myself all the time. Being Inner Directed is like controlling the weather. Outside factors don't matter. I can control my emotions by choosing my thoughts.

The degree to which you are Inner Directed or Outer Directed is reflected in your life. The consistently Inner Directed mind is focused like a laser on itself and its own process, and has much less to think about. The Outer Directed mind is very diffuse with its thinking, and has much more to think about.

The Inner Directed individual will have a much quieter life, a life that looks from the outside as if there is not much happening. This quieter life is a reflection of a quieter mind. From inside the Inner Directed mind life is experienced as that natural "**Flow**." Resolutions present themselves with relative ease in comparison to what happens elsewhere.

The other thing that happens when you are Inner Directed is that you have much more mental and physical energy. The energy that was being used diffusely when you were Outer Directed gets freed up and can be refocused. The freed up energy can be refocused to connect with your Inner Guide to develop creative and helpful solutions to any problems.

In my description of the student who got hired working 9-1 daily I mentioned that, "I immediately knew what had happened." That is because I have noticed that in my mind I can identify the difference between an answer that is coming from my ego versus an answer coming from my Inner Guide.

Of course your next question is, "What is the difference that I notice between answers from my ego and answers from my Inner Guide?" I am going to give you one of those "guru sitting on a mountain top" type answers: I find it very difficult to describe the difference between the two types of answers with words. It seems to be something that must be experienced not understood and therefore hard to describe.

This idea of not being able to use words to describe something is a valuable idea. When we experience something peaceful that words cannot describe we have experienced direct contact with our Inner Guidance.

Remember that I wrote earlier that your Inner Guide is unique in that it understands your struggles but does not allow that understanding to shift its purity. Although your Inner Guide has an existence beyond words, it knows that we operate and make decisions based on thinking with words. Therefore your Inner Guide can use words to communicate with you even though its existence is wordless. Of course it also communicates to you through feelings and wordless ideas. Your Inner Guide is able to operate in both venues, ours (using words) and it's own (wordless "knowing").

You can see how direct contact with Inner Guidance would be difficult to describe using words since it is a wordless world of "knowing." I can tell you that one byproduct of receiving Inner Guidance and a sign that you are getting information from your Inner Guide is peace. There is a sense of peace that surrounds ideas/answers that come from Inner Guidance.

So, how will you know if you are connecting with your Inner Guide? You will experience a sense of peace that is difficult to describe with words. People will ask, "How do you know this is the right thing to do?" Your answer will be something like, "I don't know, it just feels right." or "I **know** it is the answer, trust me." This can also be described as a state of Grace.

The development of ones relationship with Inner Guidance continues over time with dedication to the process of living a peaceful life. It might begin with asking for answers to questions and solutions to daily problems. As the story above illustrates, eventually I have begun to recognize there is no problem that I can't turn over to my Inner Guide and have resolved.

This idea goes way beyond just getting guidance on how to resolve difficulties. It is now the idea that I can give my difficulties to my Inner Guide and have them taken care of. It is like having the ultimate personal assistance. I just ask to have the problem taken care of and it gets resolved. The idea that I can offer difficulties up to my Inner Guide and have them resolved with no effort on my part is taking the Guided Life to another level. The following is just such a story.

My wife and I had been concerned about the school that my children attended. The details do not matter but suffice to say we were looking to put our children into another school situation the following year. We looked at private schools, charter schools, and other public schools. My wife was much more concerned about our children's current situation than I was. But, I recognized how important it was to my wife so it was important to me and I worked with her to look at alternatives.

We spent several months visiting schools and researching options. Since this process took us several months you can imagine that we ran into quite a few dead ends, schools that just didn't fit. We were not always in agreement about our assessment of each option. One night we discussed our frustration with not finding the right school. We also discussed that we needed to let go, let our Inner Guide help us resolve this situation, with complete faith that it could do so.

Sometime in the next few weeks my wife called me and said, "I visited Princeton elementary school today and met with the principal and I was really impressed….." I cut her off at this point and said, "That is where the kids need to go." She was a little taken aback by my sudden vote of confidence in a school I knew next to nothing about. She asked why I was so certain considering I had not visited and she had not given any details about her visit. My answer was that it felt right. I was getting guidance that this was the correct choice. I then told her to give me the rest of the details of her visit. I did not need the details. The decision had already been made by my Inner Guide. To make a long story short my children ended up attending this public elementary school in our residential school district.

As you are probably aware test scores are all the rage when it comes to assessing a schools ability to educate our children. It turned out that Princeton's scores were not good. Despite the concern my wife had about the test scores we sent our children there because I was guided to understand it was the right choice (and of course my wife liked the new principal and was impressed with the atmosphere at the school).

At the time of this writing my children have been attending Princeton for two school years and are having a wonderful time and getting an excellent education. Oh yeah, new test scores came out and Princeton had the largest upswing of scores in our district and is now one of the top performing schools in the district.

At the time we decided to send our children to Princeton I was not thinking about test scores, nor was I concerned about our decision. I certainly did not think to myself, "Self, don't worry, Princeton's test scores will improve dramatically very soon." But, the improvement in test scores certainly helped to reinforce my belief that Inner Guidance is the best type of guidance. It far exceeds any intellectual process I have ever experienced.

This is an example of the myriad ways in which I lean on my Inner Guide when I experience any thing that looks like a problem. Keep in mind that this chapter is titled "Taking Personal Responsibility", a necessary first step if you are going to eventually turn your life over to your Inner Guide and rely on it for directing your life.

Naturally your next questions would be "Chris, since you have learned to turn problems over to your Internal Guide, does this mean that you don't have problems anymore?" The answer is no. I still have what my ego would call problems. This is because I have not yet become a completely conscious person. My subconscious is still running the show to some extent.

Remember, the subconscious mind is filled with guilt and fear so if it is still running any portion of my mind I will see problems in my life. I have been told, and I believe, that a fully conscious person will have fewer problems but they also won't perceive anything as a problem. I am aware of that perception growing in my mind. I have fewer problems and I also perceive fewer things as problems.

Toolbox of ideas for Inner Guidance

1. Inner guidance trumps any other guidance.

2. Learning the language of Inner Guidance takes practice like learning a foreign language. Your Inner Guide is pure.

3. Your Inner Guide is **ALWAYS** broadcasting its message of peace. You need only to tune in.

4. Patience, less judgment and acceptance are mindsets that help you to match the frequency of your Inner Guide.

5. Pay attention to what thoughts bring you closer to Inner Guidance and repeat them as often as possible.

6. You must unlearn the language of judgment and learn the language of acceptance.

7. Your Inner Guide is the best judge of what is good for you!!

8. Acknowledging that you "Don't Know" what is best for you, opens you up to your Inner Guidance that does "Know" what is best for you.

9. You are tuned into the past because your thinking is mostly subconscious and the subconscious is filled with thoughts from the past.

10. People, things and events do not cause our feelings.

11. Your feelings are caused by **YOUR** thinking.

12. Being Inner Directed brings me closer to my Inner Guidance, being Outer Directed takes me farther from my Inner Guidance.

13. I must let go of my intellect's desire to be in control if I am to tune into my Inner Guide's broadcast.

14. You must let go of your belief that inflicting emotional punishment is the best way to help people change behaviors/evolve, this is not a frequency that your Inner Guide broadcasts on.

15. Taking personal responsibility for your feelings and choosing peaceful thoughts is a necessary first step in tuning into your Inner Guide.

Chapter 16
BELIEFS: THE DRIVING FORCE

As a reader of this book you came to it with a desire to tap into your Inner Guidance. To this point you have learned that you can shift your thinking to match the frequency of your Inner Guide. This is done in part by the practice of paying greater attention to how you think. By choosing more peaceful thoughts you are tuning into your Inner Guide's broadcast frequency.

Your Inner Guide, who is pure and never interferes with whatever broadcast you are choosing to listen to broadcasts on the "Present" frequency. The subconscious mind's processing of guilt and fear and its preoccupation with the past makes it difficult to think peacefully and/or in the present.

It is a beautiful thing to be aware of the idea that you can control your thinking and your mood and that by choosing peaceful loving thoughts you can increase your connection with your Inner Guidance. There is another obstacle that must be addressed before you will truly open up the communication lines to your Inner Guide.

The biggest and most deeply seated obstacle to tuning into Inner Guidance is your thoughts about yourself, or beliefs about yourself.

Keep in mind that the vast majority of your thinking is subconscious and about yourself. In fact the vast majority of your thoughts, both conscious and sub conscious are about yourself.

I once had a student tell me that he had received a phone call from a friend that he had not heard from in 5 years. Think about how you might experience such an event. I personally would be excited to catch up with an old friend and be happy that he thought to contact me after all these years.

My student was very angry about this phone call. He couldn't believe that this person had not contacted him for 5 years. Where had he been and why hadn't he stayed in touch with him. In my students mind this person's lack of contact for 5 years was an indication of how little this old friend cared about him.

Why did my student react this way? It was because he had run the situation through the filter of his self-image or self-belief. He was very lonely and felt that no one cared about him. He identified this belief as "I am all alone." It did not matter why this person had not called for 5 years. My student, like all of us, perceived situations in a way that matched his beliefs about himself.

We can also call my student's "I am all alone" belief, his **Driving Force**.

What does it mean to call someone's self belief their Driving Force? It means that a person's thoughts and actions are driven by what they believe about themselves. Before someone acts they have a thought that prompts that action. All of our thoughts are run through the filter of our beliefs about ourselves.

If I think of myself as stupid I will perceive stupidity everywhere. This is a regular occurrence in my classroom. Students arrive from a typical high school with failing grades and usually behind in credits. You can imagine that most of them think of themselves as stupid. They see their peers doing fine in high school and they are failing and they answer the question, "Why?" with "I must be stupid." My students describe things as "Stupid" regularly. They also make what you and I would consider stupid choices regularly. I know this is occurring because they are projecting their self-image onto the world.

Because my student was so very lonely and believed that no one cared about him he saw this person's 5 year absence from his life as evidence that supported his belief. Most of us consciously believe that the events that occur in our lives prove to us who we are. For example, if I am constantly experiencing failed relationships and rejections from those I pursue I may see this as proof that I am unlovable.

The reality is that you have beliefs about yourself and you go out and seek the experiences and people that match the beliefs you have about yourself. You will also avoid those experiences and people that run contrary to what you believe about yourself.

This is a pretty radical concept with regard to how we typically think things work. I am positing the idea that we look for evidence in the form of our experiences in the world to confirm what we already believe about ourselves. We want to be right about our beliefs.

We will also interpret events so that they fit our view of ourselves. If I think of myself as all alone I will interpret events so that they reinforce my belief that I am all alone. That is what happened with my student who received the phone call from an old friend. In order to illuminate the point further I will give you several examples of how this system manifests itself in people's lives.

When I was 17 years old I was having lunch in my high school cafeteria with a classmate named Betty. Betty and I were clearly attracted to one another and enjoyed each others company. This casual lunchtime relationship went on for 3 or 4 weeks. Then one day Betty brought me a rose. The Sadie Hawkins dance was coming up. For my younger readers, the Sadie Hawkins dance was the dance, back in the day, when the girls were supposed to ask the boys to the dance. The tradition was that the girl would bring the boy a flower as a symbol of her affection.

Sorry to say, but after receiving that rose from Betty I never spoke to her again. I avoided her during lunch, and if I saw her coming down the hall I would duck into a hallway or classroom. On the surface this does not make any sense. I liked Betty and she liked me. She was not asking for a lifetime commitment, just a date. But I couldn't handle it.

Now Betty's friends and my buddies were all asking me, "What's the problem?" Why was I avoiding Betty like the plague and why wouldn't I go to the dance with her. From their viewpoint there was no reason to not pursue things further.

At the time, I had no conscious idea why I was behaving in this manner. I just knew that Betty's interest in me caused me to feel very uncomfortable. So, what was happening? I, like every other human, was running my experience through my personal beliefs. In this case I was filtering my experience with Betty through my belief that I was unlovable.

The unlovable belief grew in my mind throughout my childhood. One of the key experiences that helped to solidify my unlovable belief involved my father. Although I don't remember this, my mother explained how my father's relationship with his 4 sons would change significantly around the time they turned 3. My father believed that parents should stop being affectionate with their sons at the age of three or they would grow up to be a sissy.

You can imagine that a three year old would wonder, "What is wrong with me? My dad won't cuddle with me anymore." One of my subconscious answers to this question was that I must be unlovable. I did not become consciously aware of this unlovable belief until I was in my 40's.

Not only did I reject Betty's offer of interest in me, but I pursued girls that would reject me. I did this because my belief about myself was **driving** my thinking, my decisions and therefore my behavior. The world was not proving to me that I was unlovable. I was seeking experiences that would validate how I already felt about myself. Rejecting Betty and pursuing girls that would reject me was the perfect scenario for me to be able to subconsciously validate my unlovable belief. It was also a comfort zone for me, I was comfortable experiencing the life of an unlovable person.

Remember this is all happening on a subconscious level. My unlovable story with Betty is a classic example of someone's behavior being driven by a belief that they we're unaware of. You can see that in my unlovable story and the stories that follow.

Tony Senf and I identified a woman we thought would be a great mentor for our young students in the Out of the Matrix class. We approached her and asked her to take on this role for us. In the moment, she was a little taken aback by the invitation. But, in short order she screwed on a happy face and listened to our proposal. She said she would get back to us.

At the time we made this proposal she had been attending our weekly Teen sessions for several months. After making the proposal to her I did not see her for two years. She stopped attending any and all Out of the Matrix functions even though she had been a dedicated student for more than 6 months.

This young lady did the same thing that I did with Betty. Tony's and my expression of confidence in her leadership ability did not fit with her beliefs about herself. She chose to disappear rather than try and work with Tony and me on a task she did not believe she was capable of accomplishing successfully. I know this because when I happened to run into her two years later we discussed why she disappeared and she agreed with my assessment of the situation.

The belief that was driving her decision at that time was that she was "not good enough". It did not matter that Tony and I believed in her and would support her in her efforts. Her behavior was being **driven** by her "I am not good enough" belief.

As you can imagine, once you understand this dynamic you will start to see it everywhere. That is: people making choices that are clearly not in their best interest. Whereas, in the past I did not understand why people (including myself) made self-destructive decisions, now I know that it is because they have beliefs about themselves and their decisions are born from those beliefs and not necessarily from what is in their best interest. The following is a stark example of someone whose beliefs were **driving** their behavior.

My student Brad, whose story opened this book, attended numerous Out of the Matrix weekends. It turns out that Brad is a natural presenter. He knows how to offer ideas in a thoughtful way that captures the audience's attention, as well as being charismatic. Because of this quality Brad began to do some presenting at our Out of the Matrix weekends. The adult students and mentors were very impressed with Brad and told him so.

In the middle of one of these weekends Brad came to me shaking with anxiety. "I have got to get out of here", he tells me. I asked what the problem was. Why was he feeling so anxious and needing to run away? He could not posit an answer. I pulled him into a side room and we talked about what was going on. In about 5 minutes Brad realized that all the compliments that people were paying him were making him feel anxious. "They keep telling me I am wonderful and how impressed they are with me. But I don't feel wonderful and the compliments are making me feel uncomfortable to the point where I want to run and hide. I feel like a big fake, like I am living a lie."

This was such a wonderful experience for both Brad and me. In talking through his feelings with me, Brad's anxiety disappeared and he stayed for the rest of the weekend. He realized that the anxiety was linked to his belief that he was "not good enough".

Like me with Betty, Brad couldn't handle people offering him the idea that he was something that he did not believe about himself, that he was "terrific". But, once the process became conscious, Brad knew what was happening. He was able to shift his thinking and find peace within himself.

I mentioned this was a wonderful experience for Brad and me. It was wonderful for Brad because he was able to have a real life experience of shifting his perception/thinking about a situation that caused him major anxiety.

It was wonderful for me on several levels. One because I witnessed a student and friend shift into a state of peace. I also witnessed a transformation, the transformation of a mind from being a subconscious reactor to a conscious decision maker. In the end his behavior was not being **driven** by a subconscious belief, he was making a conscious choice about his behavior.

The most amazing part was how quickly Brad was able to shift. Our private conversation lasted less than 5 minutes. Keep in mind that Brad understood much of what is presented in this book and was therefore able to make a conscious choice to experience people's compliments in way that left him in peace not anxiety.

It is that understanding, born from months of work on this material, and Brad's willingness to be Inner Directed that helped him make a shift in less than 5 minutes.

Most of the people in the world are **driven** by their subconscious beliefs *most* of the time, just like the people in the above examples. I would love to tell you that after one experience like Brad's you will never behave based on subconscious beliefs anymore. But, habits take some time to break. If you have spent your entire life subconsciously reacting to events in your life, it will take some time to break that habit, just as it will take some time to break the habit of allowing subconscious beliefs to drive your behavior.

Brad stopped working directly with Out of the Matrix a few months after the weekend in which he shifted his experience of people's compliments. He went on to pursue other interests. At the age of 20 he found himself working in an auto parts store.

You will recall that in the story that opened the book I described Brad as a wonderful 16 year old who was engaging, intelligent, hardworking, handsome and funny and A COMPLETE MESS. Hopefully you understand that description a little better now. On the surface Brad looked great and that is how you would experience him if you met him. But, his beliefs about himself created a life that was a disaster.

Well you can imagine what the folks at the auto parts store thought of him. They were amazed by this dynamic, intelligent and hard working 20 year old. They quickly started to give him more responsibility and identified him as a potential star in their company. He was quickly promoted to a shift supervisor.

At first Brad was flattered by the acknowledgment of his work ethic. But they just kept upping the ante on Brad. They decided to put him into their management trainee program. Turns out that you had to be 21 in order to enter this program, but they were so impressed with Brad they were going to make him the first 20 year old to enter this program.

Well this was just too much. Brad couldn't take it anymore. He called me several weeks after he had been offered a spot in the management trainee program. He wanted to know why he was all of a sudden calling off sick from work even though he felt fine and showing up late regularly. He said everything was going fine until they identified him as a potential management trainee. He was aware that his entire attitude about work shifted after he was tagged as a star. He said, "I just don't understand what is happening."

As Brad described the situation I was immediately taken back three years to the Out of the Matrix weekend when he got in touch with his anxiety about compliments. The situation sounded the same to me. Brad was not connecting the dots though. I walked him through what I was hearing and the connections that were occurring in my mind. He was shocked, but absolutely agreed that he was sabotaging his opportunity with this company. Their compliments were running contrary to Brad's beliefs about himself.

He and I laughed about how he was okay with the praise at first but they kept upping the ante until he felt uncomfortable.

Just as he did at that Out of the Matrix weekend as soon as he became consciously aware of what was happening Brad started to make different choices. This is another example of someone who shifted from being a subconscious reactor to external stimuli to a conscious decision maker.

Brad's story is a great illustration of how deeply seated are our beliefs about ourselves. We will not be able to overcome these beliefs and their effect on our behavior with one experience of shifting to a conscious choice maker. We will need to do it repeatedly until it is more a habit to be conscious than subconscious.

One other general example of the idea that we perceive things in a way that matches our self image is Anorexia. Anorexics see themselves as fat despite what anyone else tells them or the obvious evidence from the mirror or the scale. The self image they hold in their mind is driving their choices and therefore their behavior no matter how self-destructive the behavior may be.

One might view Anorexia as an extreme example. But, if you really think about it, there is little difference between an Anorexic seeing themselves as fat when they are skinny, or Brad thinking he is worthless when everyone else finds him valuable. The comparison ends when we take into account that Anorexia is a life threatening mental illness.

Of course we need to tie this back to our Inner Guide. All this work on becoming a conscious choice maker rather than a reactor to subconscious beliefs helps with living a more peaceful life. As you are well aware by now a more peaceful life helps with tuning in more closely to your Inner Guide's broadcast.

The stories in this chapter help to illuminate the idea that much of our behavior is being driven by beliefs in our subconscious mind. As you work to live a more peaceful life in order to expand your awareness of your Inner Guidance, identifying your false self-beliefs is a valuable process. It allows you to become a conscious choice maker about your feelings rather than a subconscious reactor to external stimuli.

Once we begin to take responsibility for our own feelings it is usually relatively easy to choose not to get upset about some rather innocuous situations like being cut off in traffic or having the cashier at the pharmacy being rude towards us. These tend to be somewhat easy situations to practice shifting your thinking and experiencing how that affects your emotions.

When we have an upset where we find it difficult to shift to peaceful thoughts, the issue is touching on our belief system about ourselves. As described earlier we **all** have beliefs about ourselves that leave us feeling something other than peace and love. **Remember all events in the life of each human being are filtered through that human being's self perception.** With that as an understanding you can see why people who regularly feel poorly about themselves have a hard time enjoying any aspect of life.

Now I am going to share with you a story of a former student who visited me and how his false self-belief was effecting his behavior, just like the stories above. But, in this story I will include more detail about how our negative false beliefs can and do affect the entire path of our lives.

My former student Josh that I wrote about earlier visited me recently. He had dropped out of school several years earlier, and was now homeless and had been in and out of jail several times since he dropped out of high school. This young man had taken the Out of the Matrix program as part of our school program, and he enjoyed and understood it.

Now, before I continue with the story of my former student I must describe something that we will use later as a template for understanding human behavior in general, and Josh's behavior more specifically.

Your computer screen provides you with visual prompts that allow you to click into various programs. Of course behind the scenes there are a multitude of different programs running to support what you see on your screen. These programs running in the background are essential to the maintenance of what is in front of you on your screen. We don't notice that background programming, but it dictates the life of our computer.

Now, let's get back to Josh. Josh was reporting to me and my co-worker that he wanted a different life. That he was tired of being homeless and in trouble with the law and he would do whatever it took to get a job and start being responsible.

Josh had been asked to leave (nice way of saying he got thrown out of) nothing short of 10 different living situations in the previous 3 years. He generally refused to cooperate fully in whatever living situation he found himself. He did not like rules, people telling him what to do or having to live up to the expectations of others. This attitude was of course why he found himself homeless. No one wants a defiant, selfish, disrespectful house mate.

It was nice to hear that Josh wanted things to change for himself. My coworker and I started to ask Josh questions about what he wanted out of life and what he needed to do to get those things. Essential to this process was Josh realizing what had gone wrong in his previous living situations. As I wrote earlier, in order to grow and develop we must learn from past mistakes and successes.

As we listened to Josh it became apparent that on one level (consciously) he had a strong desire to change and therefore change his life. But, I could hear his background program running (subconscious). As he described his previous living situations he took little responsibility for their failures. Those that he lived with were: "unfair", "liars", "too strict", and "did not understand me" and the list went on.

I explained to Josh that it was possible that in all of the 10 plus situations he had been living in, the responsibility for the failure was rarely his. But I knew Josh from his days in our school and his struggle was always around the inability to conform to the rules, whether it was in school or at home. There was little question that he continued this struggle after leaving school and it was affecting his ability to find a place to live.

Although up front (on his computer screen) he was saying he wanted things to be different, his background program (self beliefs) was running and was going to maintain his life as it was. This background program was analogous to our subconscious false self beliefs. Josh thought of himself as bad or evil. If any of us truly want to have a significant shift in our lives we must address our background programming, our subconscious beliefs about ourselves.

I mentioned to Josh that I could hear his background program running interference with his desire to have a new life. He understood the concept, in part because of his participation in Out of the Matrix.

I explained his background program to him in some detail. You will recall that Josh had a history of significant sexual abuse as a child and that was a major factor in his level of happiness and peace of mind. Josh did not trust people and his abusive background contributed to his lack of trust. His lack of trust caused him to behave in what he felt (subconsciously) were self protective ways. The subconscious prime directive for Josh was to not get emotionally close to anyone. Remember, 90% of Josh's thinking is in his subconscious mind, which is where he deals with guilt and fear.

He believed that to trust people would lead to abuse, neglect and pain. Therefore he did not want to comply with the household or school rules because that would imply that those who made the rules could be trusted or knew better than he, what was good for him. This was translated in Josh's subconscious into a message something like this: "Only trust myself. Others are out to get me and following their guidelines would imply that they are trustworthy. No one is, so don't listen to them."

It was Josh's background program, coming out of his belief that he was bad or evil, that was covertly sabotaging his attempts to improve his life.

As you read Josh's story you can understand why he had this background program. It was a way to keep him safe, and it kept him from having close relationships with people. One of the ways Josh manifested this desire to be distant from others was by not taking care of himself. He would often go weeks without bathing or washing his clothes. By keeping people at a distance he subconsciously believed he was avoiding being taken advantage of. Problem is, in Josh's case, it led to a miserable, lonely and homeless life.

We can all change our background program. In order to do this we must first be aware that there is a background program. Just like the background program on your computer, your background program is just that, hidden in the background.

Our background programs consist mostly of our thoughts about ourselves. Anyone who has spent time around a newborn knows that we come in with some programming on board. Where that programming comes from is a topic for one of my future books. Suffice it to say, we come with some preassembled programming.

How we show up as adults depends in large part on our preassembled programming and our life experiences. Those two factors contribute to our level of happiness and peace of mind. No matter what your preassembled programming and your life experience is, recognizing the Inner Directed reality of your life will allow you to overcome those factors and increase your happiness.

Maybe you did not experience the overt abuse that Josh did as a child. But, you still have a background program. Just like Josh the vast majority of people are not aware that they have a background program or what it is.

At this point one might ask, "Does all subconscious programming contribute to unhappiness and lack of connection with my Inner Guide?" The answer is no. There are certainly some things in our subconscious that are innocuous. The memory of your third grade teacher is probably harmless. But, remember one of the functions of the subconscious mind is the processing of fear and guilt. Our Inner Guide does not think about fear and guilt. It is pure unconditional love. So the more guilt and fear in our subconscious that we can release the greater our connection with our Inner Guide.

The sum of this idea is that we need to work towards viewing ourselves in loving terms. As we move towards loving ourselves more and more we are fine tuning our receiver to pick up the broadcast of our Inner Guide.

It is important to bring up the idea of a continuum again. Our thoughts and beliefs about ourselves, and life in general, exist on a continuum. If number 1 on the continuum is, "I hate myself and life in general and I am ready to commit suicide" then number 10 is "I think of myself in unconditionally loving terms all the time." We move up and down on the continuum based on our thinking in any one moment. For instance I may feel like a 6 at work where I think of myself as successful, accomplished and well liked. At home where my wife and I constantly fight, my children continually struggle with maintaining appropriate behavior then I would think of me as an ineffectual father and I would feel like a 2.

The idea that our beliefs about ourselves exist on a continuum and that they move up and down on the continuum throughout our day is important. It lets us know that the beliefs are not static, they can and do change. This in combination with the reality that I am in control of my thinking means that I can choose my thoughts about myself.

Undoing Your False Beliefs Through Observation

At this point you have come to understand that you have false beliefs about yourself that mostly exist in your subconscious mind. These beliefs have a profound effect on your life. The natural question that arises from this awareness is, "How can I affect a change to these beliefs." If I am running around thinking that I am "less than" others or "unlovable" and this is having a detrimental effect on my life then how can I change that?"

The first step in undoing ones false beliefs is to be aware that you have them. Next is to figure out what they are.

Once you have found out what the belief is you need to observe yourself living those beliefs. This is the equivalent of bringing light to darkness and the darkness is gone. Those false beliefs: "I am not good enough", "I am not worthy", "I am less than others", "I am not lovable", continue to exist only because they have not been exposed to the light of your conscious mind.

Observing our false beliefs in order to rid ourselves of them sounds incredibly simple and it is. But it is not necessarily easy because we are afraid of these beliefs. This fear causes you to store the beliefs in the darkness of your subconscious mind. Remember the subconscious is designed to store our guilt and fear and we have a tremendous amount of those feelings about our false beliefs. Humans naturally avoid emotional pain, including the emotional pain they feel about these beliefs. This is another primary reason why you may start to question this process and want to give up. You are going against your default programming to avoid these beliefs, simple but not necessarily easy.

When you become consciously aware of yourself living these beliefs they begin to dissipate. These beliefs in our subconscious are like a knot. If you understand the knot and how the different lengths of string are tied together then you can figure out which string to pull to undo the entire knot. But if the knot is in the dark and out of your reach you will never get it undone. Identifying the false beliefs is analogous to noticing how a string in your knot wraps around the other strings. With this awareness you can figure out how to pull the right string that that will undo the knot.

Of course it is important here to describe what this observing process looks like. So, here we go with another story.

I love baseball!! I have been coaching my son and daughter for the last few years in Tee-ball and coach pitch, both of which are not competitive in that they don't keep score. This year we stepped up to the kid pitch league where they do keep score and have playoffs.

Okay, so I have written a book all about having a peaceful mind in order to connect with your Inner Guide. This is all very lofty stuff. I have also worked at an alternative high school with students who "act out" on a regular basis and I have thus had a ton of practice keeping my peace of mind around some serious craziness. So, a bunch of 9-10 year olds playing baseball would be a piece of cake. NOT!!!

It turns out that I ended up with a great group of youngsters on our 9-10 year old team. They listened well, were respectful and for the most part were into learning about baseball. As a coach, especially of a group this young, you can't get a much better group then this one.

Their on the field performance was my struggle. I found myself getting angry when a player would make an error, strike out or any of the numerous mistakes that baseball players make. I did not get upset about every mistake but I did find myself at home thinking about how to improve performance. Of course improving performance is what a coach is supposed to do. But, I was aware that I had a lot of emotional energy around this desire to improve performance. This in combination with my on the field frustration with mistakes made me mentally step back and laugh at myself. Sometimes I would actually start laughing at my frustration while I was coaching third base. Some of the players were concerned that I was laughing at them. I assured them that was not the case.

Because of my emotional energy around the baseball team and its performance I knew there was something in my subconscious that was causing me some emotional pain. I allowed myself to have these feelings and minimized the judgment I had about them. In this way I was able to be more of a neutral observer of myself. "Hmm, isn't this interesting. I get worked up about a little league baseball game. I wonder what this is all about."

I also turned to my Inner Guide and asked to have whatever the issue was that was **driving** my thinking, emotions and behavior, resolved.

The season wrapped up several weeks later and I found myself very upset that we did not win the league championship. I am sophisticated enough to look good with my upsets. I did not rant or rave, cry or yell, but I found myself obsessing about the next season and what I was going to do to assure victory. I again observed my experience and noted the strong emotions I was having.

A few weeks later I was on vacation and wasn't even thinking about baseball when it occurred to me why I had so much emotional energy about the baseball team. As a youngster I experienced baseball as my salvation. I grew up in a not so happy family and baseball was an oasis for me. I was a very good baseball player and got much praise for my performance. As you may have imagined my father also loved baseball and I certainly made an association in my mind that my father would love me or love me more if I was a good baseball player.

There are many more details with regard to my relationship with baseball but suffice to say that being successful in baseball carried a lot of weight in my mind. These thoughts are of course running around in my subconscious and it took this experience with the little league team to bring it up for me. I recognized that my overreaction to the little league games was due to my strong association with baseball success and my desire to feel loved.

The important lesson here is that by observing yourself getting upset, like an impartial third party, you open yourself up to healing. This impartial process works like this: You get upset. You choose not to judge yourself for your upset. This keeps you in a peaceful state of mind and therefore connected to your Inner Guide since it is broadcasting on the peace of mind network. You are then able to get information from your Inner Guide that will help you to heal.

Remember, you have emotional pain running around in your subconscious and you can be assured that your upsetting emotions that show up today are about emotional pain related to your long held false negative beliefs. This is pain that you naturally retreat from. Know that you have pain, be okay with the fact that you have pain (don't judge) and it will be much easier to release. If you live in denial and won't acknowledge that you have emotional pain it will remain as your subconscious **Driving Force**.

You need practice at being that impartial (non-judgmental) observer of your upsets. I am including some writing prompts in order to facilitate that impartial process. The end goal here is to identify some of your false beliefs so that you can consciously observe yourself having feelings and making decisions that are generated by those beliefs.

If you would like worksheets that include all the instructions that follow, you can visit my website, www.chrislauretig.com and click on the worksheets tab.

The Beliefs Awareness Process

Make sure you read all the instructions before you begin.

Step One: Pick an upsetting situation or person in your life. Take some time to write out exactly what it is you are upset about. Possible topics can include but are not limited to: Boss doesn't respect me, child doesn't listen to me, my wife drinks too much, my car is always breaking down, I don't have enough money.

These are times when you are being Outer Directed, believing that something outside of you is causing your upset. Write a detailed description of the situation. You will not need to show this to anyone so don't hold back.

I would encourage you to choose the individual/situation you have the greatest emotional charge around. More often than not this will be someone close to you such as a family member. You will get the greatest bang for your buck by picking the situation that upsets you the most.

You may not like this, but if you come to this point and think, "I really don't have anything or anyone that upsets me", you are in some level of denial. Most everyone on the planet has some things that upset them. If you are having a hard time here are a few alternative suggestions to get you started: The weather, the school system, taxes, the local sports team, politics or a politician, an illness. I still believe that something closer to home like your spouse, parent, child, best friend, boss will garner a greater impact but in the end an upset is an upset.

Step Two: Next write out what you would like to say to the individual/situation that is upsetting you. Don't hold back on this one either. Really get into the feelings and express them on the paper.

Step Three: write down the feelings that come up for you around this situation, there is a list below for your reference. This should be a list of one word feelings for example: angry, frustrated, sad or depressed. Don't make the mistake of writing out "I feel like I should quit my job" or "I feel like my mother is unfair." There are no feelings listed in those sentences.

Having identified the feelings associated with this upset you have begun the process of observing yourself. You now know what feelings are associated with the upset that you have written about. For some of you that may seem like an insignificant step in the process. For others identifying feelings is a big step in the direction of self awareness.

Angry	Sad
Frustrated	Depressed
Annoyed	Enraged
Afraid	Jealous
Envious	Hateful
Bitter	Guilty
Anxious	Lonely
Unhappy	Embarrassed
Resentful	Grief

Write down any other feelings that occur to you.

Step Four: From the list below, or if you come up with a trigger not listed, pick what you believe was done to you in this upset and write it down. Even though your feelings are caused by how you think, that is not our everyday experience. We believe that someone else's behavior or an event caused our feelings. Below you will identify what you believe triggered your upsetting feelings.

Accused me	Forgot about me
Blamed me	Did not show up
Yelled at me	Made me wrong
Disrespected me	Left me
Attacked me	Ignored me
Scolded me	Criticized me
Abused me	Made fun of me
Belittled me	Laughed at me
Abandoned me	Neglected me

At this point you have identified something that upsets you, how you feel about it and what you believe was done to you to trigger your upset. Take a minute to look at what you have written and how you have understood this situation until now.

An example would be helpful here. Let's say you are angry with your wife because she isn't as interested in sex as you would like her to be. You feel angry and sad about this and you believe she is ignoring your needs and not caring about you. Until now you have believed you feel angry and sad because of your wife's behavior. I am telling you it is actually about how you think about the situation, your wife and yourself, not about your wife's behavior. With that as an example we will move onto the next steps in the process.

Step Five: Think about the event or person you are writing about and see which belief below resonates with you with respect to this upset.

I am not:	Smart enough
Cared for	Good looking enough
Lovable	Tall enough
Liked	Thin enough
Included	The right color
Worthy	The right ethnicity
Deserving	Talented enough
Important	Like everyone else
Wanted	Understood

I am:	All alone
Lonely	Left out
Not loved	Different
Stupid	worthless
Lazy	Insignificant
A screw up	Broken
Incapable	Bad
Limited	Evil
No good	Small

Keep in mind that this list is not comprehensive. If you become aware of a belief that resonates with you that is not listed here please write it down. After you have looked over the list write down the three beliefs that resonate with you the most.

Congratulations, you have just identified some false beliefs you have that are directing your life. Remember that these beliefs are maintained in your thinking because they are hidden in your subconscious mind.

By identifying them in this conscious exercise you are exposing them to the light of your conscious mind and therefore working to dissipate them. This may be uncomfortable on some level. You may even have the thought, "I can't believe that I think that I am Not Worthy." But you still feel that resonance within you that says, "I actually do believe this about myself." Stick with it even though it may be uncomfortable.

Earlier I wrote that you want to work to rid yourself of your buttons rather than trying to get everyone to stop pushing them (remember the snowflake analogy). That is what these writing exercises are designed to do, help you be aware of your subconscious beliefs so you can rid yourself of them. This is the first step in becoming a conscious choice maker rather than a subconscious reactor.

Having become consciously aware of these beliefs through these writing exercises, you will now need a way to be conscious of them throughout your day. This daily awareness process will revolve around observing yourself in the act of experiencing these buttons/beliefs getting pushed.

Now that you have identified the beliefs that direct your life you can back track to the original upset that you started these writing exercises with. Who or whatever it was that you were upset with is the thing that pushed or triggered your button (your false belief). If it is your mother, know that when you get around her you often get upset. Know that when you get upset it is because your experience of Mom is pushing your "I'm not good enough" button. You have set yourself up to be the observer. You are going into the situation consciously aware of what is going to happen.

Let's move onto the next step in this awareness exercise.

Trigger Awareness Exercise

1. Pick the belief that resonates with you and that you want to work on. You may change your mind about what belief you are working on after reading all these directions or at any time during the process if it occurs to you that you need to change things up. Be sure not to change things just because it is uncomfortable, discomfort will lead to growth. Write down the belief you are working on (this should be the one that you have the most feelings around).

Belief: _____ (Not good enough, unworthy, not smart enough, incapable, etcetera)

2. List the trigger people/circumstance/things that push this button for you. Then list the subsequent feelings that you have when this button gets pushed.

Example: I think I am Not Good Enough

Trigger	Feeling
Mother	Angry
Work	Depressed

At this time you may only be able to come up with one person or circumstance that pushes this button for you. Chances are there is more than one trigger for your false belief. As you become more consciously aware of this belief you will probably be able to add new names and circumstances to the list. For Instance you may not realize that the secretary at your office pushes your "I'm not good enough" button until you start working on the belief. Add her to the list if it fits.

What you are doing in this exercise is becoming a conscious observer of yourself living out this false belief. "Now I know that the angry feelings that I have when interacting with my mother are about my, "I am not good enough belief". So, when I get angry while inter-acting with Mom I will mentally note: "This is not about Mom it is about my false belief."

This simple process of consciously acknowledging what is actually happening in your mind will help to dissipate the belief. Over time you will start to notice that your reaction to the trigger people listed above will shift. Your upset will: shorten in length, lessen in intensity, not happen as frequently and/or disappear.

During this observation phase of undoing your belief there is a tendency to become overwhelmed. "I can't believe how pervasive this belief is for me. What is wrong with me?" At this point one might con-sider giving up because it seems like too much to handle. This is why I ask that you be a neutral observer of your belief in action. Notice that I am not telling you to "Judge the hell out of yourself", for having this belief. Step back and be okay with it.

This is where you will need to have a little trust and faith in this process that I am describing. Observing with as much neutrality as you can muster WILL dissipate these beliefs and their impact on your life. Of course in the process of dissipating the belief you will be clearing the way for your Inner Guide's broadcast of peace and love.

Chances are the first time you observe yourself living out this belief you will get just as upset as you had in the past. But, pay close attention and over time you will notice some subtle differences. Maybe you are not upset for as long as in the past, 2 days versus a week or your upset is not as intense.

You simply observe these beliefs having an impact on your life. Recognizing that your feelings are being generated inside of you by how you think, specifically how you think about yourself. The con-scious awareness of you acting out your beliefs will help you to undo them. Remember these beliefs are hidden (denial) in your subconscious mind. The opposite of denial is awareness and acknowledgment.

By remaining vigilant about looking for these false beliefs you are emptying your subconscious mind of guilt and fear. You will therefore be less preoccupied with guilt and fear. Being less preoccupied with guilt and fear you will be more peaceful and happy. Being more peaceful and happy you will be more closely attuned to your Inner Guide. Now you can understand why it is so important to go after your false beliefs, your subconscious guilt and fear.

Toolbox of Ideas for Inner Guidance

1. Inner guidance trumps any other guidance.

2. Learning the language of Inner Guidance takes practice like learning a foreign language. Your Inner Guide is pure.

3. Your Inner Guide is **ALWAYS** broadcasting its message of peace. You need only to tune in.

4. Patience, less judgment and acceptance are mindsets that help you to match the frequency of your Inner Guide.

5. Pay attention to what thoughts bring you closer to Inner Guidance and repeat them as often as possible.

6. You must unlearn the language of judgment and learn the language of acceptance.

7. Your Inner Guide is the best judge of what is good for you!!

8. Acknowledging that you "Don't Know" what is best for you, opens you up to your Inner Guidance that does "Know" what is best for you.

9. You are tuned into the past because your thinking is mostly subconscious and the subconscious is filled with thoughts from the past.

10. People, things and events do not cause our feelings.

11. Your feelings are caused by **YOUR** thinking.

12. Being Inner Directed brings me closer to my Inner Guidance, being Outer Directed takes me farther from my Inner Guidance.

13. I must let go of my intellect's desire to be in control if I am to tune into my Inner Guide's broadcast.

14. You must let go of your belief that inflicting emotional punishment is the best way to help people change behaviors/evolve, this is not a frequency that your Inner Guide broadcasts on.

15. Taking personal responsibility for your feelings and choosing peaceful thoughts is a necessary first step in tuning into your Inner Guide.

16. Your subconscious false beliefs about yourself are driving your thinking and behavior.

Chapter 17
PAIN AS THE GATEWAY TO PEACE

E motional pain is your gateway to attaining true inner peace and therefore true Inner Guidance. Wow! As you read that you probably had the thought, "How can emotional pain be a gateway to attaining inner peace? Isn't emotional pain the opposite of Inner Peace?"

The answer to the second question is, yes. Emotional pain is the opposite of Inner Peace. The degree of pain your mind is experiencing is in direct opposition to the amount of peace your mind is experiencing.

A more accurate statement might be that the removal or end of emotional pain leads to Inner Peace. But the removal or end of emotional pain requires that we first look at or move into the pain. People's emotional pain revolves around the false beliefs that we identified in the previous Chapter. Therefore you have already begun to look at and release your emotional pain.

Avoidance of Emotional Pain

It makes perfectly good sense that ending emotional pain would lead to Inner Peace. Unfortunately most people do not work to end their emotional pain. They simply work to avoid it.

Going from avoiding pain to examining pain and going from blaming things outside of you for your pain to acknowledging that you are causing it with your thinking, is turning your emotional world upside down. In order to make this reversal occur we must have some understanding of how we have operated to this point. If I am to reverse a process I must understand the original process so that I can take it in the opposite direction.

The first question is, "What does this avoidance of emotional pain look like? How does it function in our day to day lives?"

Let's look at an example of emotional pain. How it developed from someone's self image and therefore dictated their behavior.

The examination of emotional pain starts with an important question, to be asked when you are actively upset: "What must I be believing and therefore thinking of myself that is leaving me feeling angry/sad/ anxious frustrated, not at peace?" This question is helpful on several levels. It helps to bring you back to an Inner Directed perception that your upset is being produced inside of you. It also reminds you that any upset is related to your beliefs about yourself. By prompting yourself with this question you are quickly shifting the perception of your upset from being caused outside of you to recognizing that it is caused by your thinking, specifically your thoughts about yourself.

The question, "What must I be believing about myself that would leave me feeling this way?" is best asked with the background of already understanding your false beliefs. In other words, you are best served to have read and understood the material in this book and to have completed the writing prompts contained in chapter 16. The writing prompts help you to narrow down the field of possible beliefs that are causing your upset. Once you have identified the 3-4 main beliefs that resonate with you, then the answer to the above question is usually easily recognized in any upsetting situation.

Let's say that your father decided to stop being affectionate with you at the age of 3 (sound familiar?). Without getting into all the details this experience would have an impact on your beliefs about yourself. Children tend to think of themselves as the cause of their parents dysfunctional behavior. "What did I do to cause my dad to stop being affectionate with me?" Or "What is wrong with me that my dad doesn't love me?" We all answer these questions with statements like "I must be unlovable, unworthy, bad." The variety of answers we come up with is endless. This is what occurred to me with my father. When he stopped being affectionate with me I identified the reason as "I must not be lovable." This is a simplification, because there were many other factors in my life that contributed to this belief becoming cemented in my subconscious mind.

Now that you have identified the belief that is driving your upset you need to go through a process of letting go of your identification with that belief. Because of the process described in this book I am consciously aware that I have the "I'm Unlovable" belief and I have some idea of what people and circumstance push that button for me.

Next I look at what exactly qualifies me as "Unlovable." Was I born unlovable? Do I have the unlovable gene? What exactly is it that makes me unlovable? These questions help to establish in my mind that my biological makeup has nothing to do with this belief. As I walk myself through this process I start to recognize that the belief exists only as a thought in my mind. It has no physical reality. Yes I might have behaved in an unlovable way at some points in my life. But I have begun to recognize that the behavior was driven by the belief, the behavior did not prove the belief true.

Traditional healing would ask that you talk about the thoughts and feelings surrounding your dad so that you might lessen their impact on you. This can certainly be helpful and it is an example of identifying something emotionally painful and going against your instincts to avoid pain and instead lean into it and examine it.

I would add to this idea by helping you recognize the feelings you are having about your father are not being caused by him or his behavior. The feelings are being caused by your thinking, specifically the thoughts you have about yourself. As was mentioned earlier once you understand the idea that your emotions are produced by your thinking it opens up a whole new world to you.

You might say, "Chris, in your story you identified your father's behavior/attitude as a contributing factor to your Unlovable belief. Doesn't that mean that he is on some level the cause of the belief?" This is an excellent question. My answer is: Children's beliefs about themselves are heavily influenced by their parents. But, as an adult you can release yourself from your parents influence. You can take control of your own thinking and make a shift in your self-image or beliefs. In this way you can honestly say, "My beliefs are my beliefs and therefore I can shift them." If I continue to hold my parents responsible for my beliefs I will never be able to change them.

As we continue this examination remember that our emotional pain is stored in our subconscious mind which is a very nice system for denial. Put something in a place that I have limited awareness of. I can act as if there is not a sink full of dirty dishes. But, my denial of the dirty dishes does not change the reality nor does it get the dishes cleaned. It is the same for emotional pain. In order for the pain to get dealt with I must acknowledge it, clean it up and get rid of it, not walk around acting as if I don't have any pain (denial).

Problem is that dirty dishes hidden in the cabinet fester, smell and get down right nasty. On some level I will always know those dishes are there. It works the same with emotional pain. It may be hidden in my subconscious but it will sit there, fester and some part of me will always know that it is there, until I come up with a system to acknowledge and rid myself of this pain. In order to clean up this emotional pain I will need to go against my natural inclination to avoid pain.

"I have a natural inclination to avoid emotional pain?" Yes, not only are we wired to avoid physical pain. We are wired to avoid emotional pain. We touch the hot stove and understand we don't want to do that anymore. We touch into an emotionally painful memory/ thought and we avoid it like the hot stove. We don't like to feel emotional pain!! That's a shocker. That is one of those incredibly obvious statements like, "Water is wet."

All of this means that the entre into a more peaceful life begins with seeking out our emotional pain. It seems counterintuitive that we should seek out something that we don't like and is painful in order to live a more peaceful life. But look at the common sense nature of the fact that if I don't work to clean something up it stays dirty and undealt with and negatively impacts my life.

I don't even want to think about how many decisions I made because I wanted to avoid the pain I felt about my unlovable belief. I was not aware of my subconscious, conscious or anything else at 17. I just knew emotional pain and subconsciously worked hard to avoid it.

I go back to an awareness I wrote about earlier in order to sell you on this idea of seeking out your pain in order to rid yourself of it. We must learn by contrast. I have spent much of my life avoiding my personal pain, and it simply leads to more and more misery. I have spent a shorter period of my life seeking out my pain in order to rid myself of it. The growth in the level of peace I have experienced since I reversed my inclination to avoid pain is tremendous. This is the ultimate evidence that seeking out the pain to rid myself of it is the path to peace.

It is also important to point out that I am not referring to identifying the cause of my pain and then reveling in it. I am speaking of identifying it so that the light of my conscious mind can help to dissipate it. This means that I know my subconscious thinking is the cause and the retainer of my pain. I therefore work to make that thinking conscious so that I can work to release it.

I don't ask that you believe me. But, I do ask that you spend some time and effort seeking out your pain. Use that experience as a litmus test. If you experience greater peace then you will be sold on the idea of seeking out your pain.

Here is another radical notion. Because humans naturally avoid emotional pain, most people's lives are organized around the avoidance of emotional pain. They make day to day decisions and in fact their entire lives are designed to help them avoid their emotional pain. Every decision they have ever made was heavily influenced by the desire to avoid their emotional pain.

Let's take a minute to examine this idea that people's entire lives are designed around a desire to avoid emotional pain. Remember that 90% of our thinking is subconscious and that our subconscious is where we store our guilt and fear (emotional pain). Factor in that humans are wired to avoid pain and you can see how people's lives would revolve around the theme of avoiding pain, and they wouldn't even be aware that that is what is happening.

The idea in the previous paragraph may be difficult to believe. I did not come to believe it until I began working the process described in this book for living a more peaceful and Guided life. A helpful analogy might be dieting. Have you noticed that when you make a choice to eat a healthier diet you are much more aware of the unhealthy eating habits of others? It is the same with this process of addressing your emotional pain in order to live a more peaceful life. Once you start the process of looking at **your** pain you begin to notice how much energy other people are exerting to avoid their own.

You certainly don't need to believe in the idea that people's lives are designed around the need to avoid their pain. Whether you believe that assertion or not you can still work to live a more peaceful life for the benefits it will bring to your life.

Releasing Emotional Pain

There is an important distinction that needs to be made here. One might look at a traditional healing method for pursuing and releasing emotional pain. There are a few differences in how traditional healing pursues emotional pain and what I am proposing. The beginning is very similar, acknowledging that I have pain and getting a description of what is the cause of the pain. The two methods quickly diverge after this.

Traditional healing methods would often help you to see the cause of your upset as outside of you, your mom or dad, your spouse, your boss, your children etcetera. All Outer Directed. Your coach in this process might then offer you some ideas and techniques for dealing with the upsetting person/situation. I would alternatively propose that the cause of your upset is your thinking, which is linked to how you perceive yourself. Inner Directed. I would then walk you through how you could think about yourself differently and therefore see the other person/situation differently leaving you in peace.

I believe that this method is cutting right to the chase by addressing your beliefs about yourself and your subsequent thoughts. Since your feelings are produced in your hypothalamus by your thinking you cut out the middleman (parent, spouse, child, boss, etcetera), and recognize, "I produce my feelings with how I think. How can I think about myself in this situation differently so I can be at peace?"

Once you have shifted to an Inner Directed perception and recognize that it is your beliefs that are driving your upset and your behavior, you perceive what is happening outside of you differently. You will be much more likely to quickly shift to a peaceful state of mind because you will not need the circumstances outside of you to change.

Here is a quick reminder. This process will happen with varying degrees of rapidity depending on whom and what you are dealing with. The reason I have indicated that you might want to go after the upsets with those close to you is because those interactions are most likely to tap into your beliefs. This is the case because those close to you have probably helped to maintain and grow these beliefs in you.

Toolbox of ideas for Inner Guidance

1. Inner guidance trumps any other guidance.

2. Learning the language of Inner Guidance takes practice like learning a foreign language. Your Inner Guide is pure.

3. Your Inner Guide is **ALWAYS** broadcasting its message of peace. You need only to tune in.

4. Patience, less judgment and acceptance are mindsets that help you to match the frequency of your Inner Guide.

5. Pay attention to what thoughts bring you closer to Inner Guidance and repeat them as often as possible.

6. You must unlearn the language of judgment and learn the language of acceptance.

7. Your Inner Guide is the best judge of what is good for you!!

8. Acknowledging that you "Don't Know" what is best for you, opens you up to your Inner Guidance that does "Know" what is best for you.

9. You are tuned into the past because your thinking is mostly subconscious and the subconscious is filled with thoughts from the past.

10. People, things and events do not cause our feelings.

11. Your feelings are caused by **YOUR** thinking.

12. Being Inner Directed brings me closer to my Inner Guidance, being Outer Directed takes me farther from my Inner Guidance.

13. I must let go of my intellect's desire to be in control if I am to tune into my Inner Guide's broadcast.

14. You must let go of your belief that inflicting emotional punishment is the best way to help people change behaviors/evolve, this is not a frequency that your Inner Guide broadcasts on.

15. Taking personal responsibility for your feelings and choosing peaceful thoughts is a necessary first step in tuning into your Inner Guide.

16. Your subconscious false beliefs about yourself are driving your behavior.

17. Overcome your natural inclination to avoid your emotional pain and instead examine it and understand it so that you can release it and therefore be more peaceful.

Chapter 18
PURPOSE

All that has been described thus far needs a booster shot. It is all very good information and can be used at minimum to create a happier more peaceful life for you. At maximum it can work to continuously expand your connection with your Inner Guidance. But there is one mindset that will boost this process over the top for you.

The booster shot is "Purpose". The right Purpose for your life will help you to more finely tune into your Inner Guide. Of course if we are to choose a Purpose that will allow us to tune more finely into our Inner Guidance we need to understand "Purpose" as a concept.

Purpose is the defining or guiding principle that directs our thinking as well as our actions. Most people don't consciously consider what their Purpose is in life. Despite that, you can see various Purposes going on out there in people's lives. This may include: Helping others, making money, garnering fame, living longer and the list goes on and on.

As you review and think about the ideas expressed in this book I hope a few things have become apparent too you. The first thing is that we have spent a tremendous amount of energy working to protect ourselves from our emotional pain. This idea was addressed in the previous chapter. In fact I posited the idea that Avoidance of Emotional Pain is most humans' primary Purpose in life. I believe this is in part because of what I understand about our subconscious mind and its focus on guilt and fear.

Think about the definition of Purpose, a defining or guiding principle in our minds that drives our behavior/choices. Combine that with the idea that most of our thinking is subconscious (90%). Then consider that most people do not consciously choose a Purpose for their lives. Would it be unreasonable then to think that most people's Purpose is being developed from their subconscious thinking? In other words our Purpose is being primarily directed by thinking that we are not aware of.

One must be aware of the ideas in the previous paragraph so that we do not end up with a default Purpose we are not aware of. The only way to avoid having your subconscious thinking direct your Purpose in life is to **consciously** choose a Purpose, and then have a method of pursuing that Purpose.

Let's take this a step farther. Our subconscious deals with the past and then processes our guilt and fear. We now start to see a picture emerge of people's Purpose in life being developed out of a system that focuses on guilt and fear from the past, and they are unaware that this process is happening. You can see why I believe that most people's primary purpose in life is to avoid their emotional pain. This of course means that most people's Purpose immediately tunes them out of their Inner Guide's broadcast on the Peace and love frequency.

Wanting to live The Guided Life means that we want to consciously choose our Purpose. Not having our Purpose come from default programming in our subconscious mind. This is similar to our foreign language analogy from earlier in the book. One of the methods we must employ to overcome the subconscious Purpose to avoid pain is to consciously choose a different Purpose. Just like needing to consciously choose the French word for "Chair" as a native English speaker. Our default "language" is to avoid our emotional pain. We must consciously choose our "new language" which is examining our Pain.

On the surface it would seem that the avoidance of emotional pain is a pretty good Purpose. Who wants to experience emotional pain? Unfortunately, the Purpose of avoiding emotional pain keeps us stuck in a cycle of thinking and behavior that is driven by subconscious thoughts. When you look at the Purpose of avoiding emotional pain from the perspective that it causes us to behave subconsciously it looks much less appealing.

Let's say that you have decided to make Peace of Mind your primary Purpose in life. Just stating this is not enough. It will be a much more effective Purpose if you know how to implement a process to increase your peace of mind. If I have the Purpose of writing a book I must first know how to read and write. It is the same for Peace of Mind. You need a system to implement in order to pursue your Purpose.

There are two significant understandings with respect to your emotional pain. First is that you create it with how you think. Remember the hypothalamus is triggered to release its emotional chemicals by your thinking. The second is that your painful thinking revolves around your beliefs about yourself. Both of these ideas have been addressed extensively earlier in the book. The mind training tools in this book are the process you can use to release your emotional pain.

To this point in my life, pursuing and releasing my pain has been the most effective method I have discovered for increasing my peace of mind. I am also aware that the pain has diminished significantly over time. In other words I am getting to a tipping point where although I am seeking out my pain, there is less of it to be found. As you have a more peaceful mind you will find that your experience of everything, including things and people that you have been interacting with for years, will shift.

When I was in my mid thirties I stopped over to my parent's house to visit. I was there for several hours with both my mom and dad. Upon leaving that day I was aware of a very different sensation. I sat in my car for a few minutes and realized that I actually enjoyed being around my father. It was pleasant! I also recognized that up until that day I hated my father and being around him made my skin crawl. I consciously knew that I had anger issues with my dad. But until that day I did not realize to what degree.

I could not remember ever feeling warm pleasant feelings about my dad. It really struck me on that day because I could contrast how I felt leaving that day, with how I had felt for as long as I could remember. But until I had this pleasant day I was not aware of how unpleasant it had been. Being unhappy and angry around my dad had become the norm. It was so normal for me that I did not even know it was happening. I just thought that was the way it was. I did not recognize that it could be different. I needed the contrasting experience of a pleasant time with Dad to recognize how unpleasant things had been. At that point in my life I had done years of work on myself in various therapeutic situations. Although I had done very little direct work on my relationship with my father. On that fateful day I had done enough internal work on my beliefs that my father's presence did not push my "I'm not lovable" button. By the way, it was not that my father did anything different. My button had shrunk and was much less likely to get pushed by anyone.

This is what I tell folks who come to me with upsetting situations/people in their lives. "Your button (belief) is getting pushed. Let's work to rid you of the button rather than going around making sure no one pushes your button." This is like the analogy I told earlier about the snowflakes. It is much easier (it is possible) to shrink your negative beliefs/buttons, rather then trying to get everyone to stop pushing that button (impossible).

I did years and years of work on my self before I had that pleasant day with my dad. Those years of work were not specifically targeted on my "Unlovable" belief. I actually did not identify the specifics of the belief until years later when I got familiar with the techniques described in this book.

To state the obvious, releasing ones buttons/beliefs is much easier when one can identify the buttons. I am sure that if I had gotten aware of my "Unlovable" belief I would have healed much more quickly than I did. This is why I encourage you to work the beliefs identification process in this book so that you can more quickly release these beliefs and therefore release their effects on your life.

Once you have decided that Peace of Mind is your Purpose in life your interactions with others will start to shift. You will begin to seek out and find more peace in all aspects of the world. A beautiful side effect of having the Purpose of Peace of Mind is that you will help to facilitate Peace of Mind for others. Be careful with this idea. Your ego will want to take on facilitating the Peace of Mind for others as your Purpose, which is Outer Directed.

There is a subtle difference here. When you make your own Peace of Mind the Purpose of your life you will automatically help others with their Peace of Mind without any effort on your part. You will find yourself saying things to other people that resonate with them, and they will tell you so. Whereas when your Purpose is to help others with their Peace of Mind you will find yourself frustrated with people for not shifting based on your "help."

Hopefully you are asking: "Why does helping others with their Peace of Mind occur without any effort when my Purpose is my own Peace of Mind?" Because when you are becoming more peaceful you are tuning into your Inner Guide and you will do and say things that are directed by that Inner Guide rather than your ego, such as the following story.

At the age of 7 my daughter Abigail came home from the second grade and reported to me that she had a bad day at school. This was unusual in that she almost always enjoyed school and rarely reported anything negative. Her report of a bad day was so unusual that I pursued information from her about what had happened.

She described to me an incident that took place between her and her teacher. Her teacher was upset with her for not turning in an assignment in a timely fashion. I understood my daughter's concerns especially since she liked her teacher very much and did not like her being upset with my daughter.

I went on to ask her about the rest of her school day. She described a very typical day and reported that everything else in her day went well. She even gave me some specifics about some fun things that happened.

I was then guided to point out to her that her school day consisted of 390 minutes. I also pointed out that the incident that occurred with her teacher lasted approximately one minute. She had already acknowledged that the rest of her day had gone quite well.

She is now staring wide eyed at me. Clearly wondering where I am going with all of this. I pointed out that our conversation started with her reporting to me that she had a bad day at school. But the incident that caused her to describe a bad day lasted for only 1 minute of her 390 minute school day. She immediately understood what I was explaining to her. I explained that she had a bad minute but her day was good.

She has mentioned on several occasion how she has used that method of looking at things to help her when she was feeling badly about something.

About a year later she came home to report to me that she had a bad day at school. This was still unusual for her. She recited to me about 6 things in her day that were unpleasant. Following that up immediately with, "Now dad, you can't tell me it was just one minute of my day this time!" I said, "Your right Honey." We had a good laugh and moved on with our evening together.

I am quite clear that my Purpose of Peace of Mind impacted the way I handled my daughter in this situation. This is because my Peace of Mind keeps me connected with my Inner Guide. My words are then directed by my Inner Guide not my ego and therefore impact those I am interacting with differently.

I use this technique quite frequently. As I am interacting with people I ask my Inner Guide to direct my words. As you will read in chapter 20 I call this "Checking In." After Checking In I am often surprised at what comes out of my mouth. In the scenario with my daughter you might think that I had the idea of describing her day to her in this way before I ever spoke to her. Not so, as is often the case with Guided comments they occur to me in the moment and after I have made them I think to myself, "Wow that was a great way to put things."

THERE WILL COME A TIME...

After making Peace of Mind your Purpose and working the process described in this book there will come a time when you will no longer need to consciously work to contact your Inner Guide. Your mind will be operating on a level of peace that you will find yourself in regular contact with your Inner Guide, Effortlessly! Inner Guidance has become your default language. You are no longer subconsciously reacting to external stimuli. Instead you have turned your life over to your Inner Guide. This purveyor of Peace is now your primary form of support in this world.

Toolbox of ideas for Inner Guidance

1. Inner guidance trumps any other guidance.
2. Learning the language of Inner Guidance takes practice like learning a foreign language. Your Inner Guide is pure.
3. Your Inner Guide is **ALWAYS** broadcasting its message of peace. You need only to tune in.
4. Patience, less judgment and acceptance are mindsets that help you to match the frequency of your Inner Guide.
5. Pay attention to what thoughts bring you closer to Inner Guidance and repeat them as often as possible.
6. You must unlearn the language of judgment and learn the language of acceptance.
7. Your Inner Guide is the best judge of what is good for you!!
8. Acknowledging that you "Don't Know" what is best for you, opens you up to your Inner Guidance that does "Know" what is best for you.
9. You are tuned into the past because your thinking is mostly subconscious and the subconscious is filled with thoughts from the past.
10. People, things and events do not cause our feelings.
11. Your feelings are caused by **YOUR** thinking.
12. Being Inner Directed brings me closer to my Inner Guidance, being Outer Directed takes me farther from my Inner Guidance.
13. I must let go of my intellect's desire to be in control if I am to tune into my Inner Guide's broadcast.
14. You must let go of your belief that inflicting emotional punishment is the best way to help people change behaviors/evolve, this is not a frequency that your Inner Guide broadcasts on.
15. Taking personal responsibility for your feelings and choosing peaceful thoughts is a necessary first step in tuning into your Inner Guide.

16. Your subconscious false beliefs about yourself are driving your behavior.

17. Overcome your natural inclination to avoid your emotional pain and instead examine it and understand it so that you can release it and therefore be more peaceful.

18. Do not allow your purpose in life to be driven by your subconscious thinking, make a conscious decision to make Peace of Mind your Purpose in life.

Chapter 19
TRACKING YOUR PROGRESS

In chapter two I wrote that we must learn from our past mistakes in order to correct them. In this same vein you will know you are making progress on this path of living a guided life by comparing your current experiences with past experiences.

For our purposes this method of comparison is specific to the things that upset you. Remember the goal is to have a more peaceful mind so that you can tune into Inner Guidance. Being less upset will lead to greater Peace of Mind.

As you work the processes described in this book you will know you are making progress when you can witness yourself returning to your peace of mind more quickly than in the past. In other words something that used to upset you for days only upsets you for a few hours. Because we have a tendency to emotionally beat ourselves up we might see returning to our peace of mind in a few hours as not good enough. This is why it is important to compare your current experience to the past. Going from days of upset to hours of upset is a huge, beautiful and wonderful accomplishment. Don't fall into the ego trick of expecting perfection.

To make this point as clear as possible it is helpful to give a specific example. Let's say you would see your mother once a month and be upset for several days after seeing her. Notice that now you are only upset for one day. Phenomenal, you are on your way!! Keep working the process and shortening the length of the upset and one day you will no longer allow your mother to push your buttons at all.

It is a lofty and sometimes daunting idea that I am working towards living a life of complete peace and unconditional love. It is helpful to realize that that is the end result goal that I am shooting for, but on a daily basis I simplify it for myself. This simplification is that I work to be more peaceful and loving today, and if I am more peaceful and loving today then I am working towards the end goal. I don't need to overwhelm myself with an end goal that at times can seem impossible to attain. Just do what you can do today to make your life more peaceful. A journey of a thousand miles begins with one step!!

Toolbox of ideas for Inner Guidance

1. Inner guidance trumps any other guidance.
2. Learning the language of Inner Guidance takes practice like learning a foreign language. Your Inner Guide is pure.
3. Your Inner Guide is **ALWAYS** broadcasting its message of peace. You need only to tune in.
4. Patience, less judgment and acceptance are mindsets that help you to match the frequency of your Inner Guide.
5. Pay attention to what thoughts bring you closer to Inner Guidance and repeat them as often as possible.
6. You must unlearn the language of judgment and learn the language of acceptance.
7. Your Inner Guide is the best judge of what is good for you!!
8. Acknowledging that you "Don't Know" what is best for you, opens you up to your Inner Guidance that does "Know" what is best for you.
9. You are tuned into the past because your thinking is mostly subconscious and the subconscious is filled with thoughts from the past.
10. People, things and events do not cause our feelings.
11. Your feelings are caused by **YOUR** thinking.
12. Being Inner Directed brings me closer to my Inner Guidance, being Outer Directed takes me farther from my Inner Guidance.
13. I must let go of my intellect's desire to be in control if I am to tune into my Inner Guide's broadcast.
14. You must let go of your belief that inflicting emotional punishment is the best way to help people change behaviors/evolve, this is not a frequency that your Inner Guide broadcasts on.
15. Taking personal responsibility for your feelings and choosing peaceful thoughts is a necessary first step in tuning into your Inner Guide.

16. Your subconscious false beliefs about yourself are driving your behavior.

17. Overcome your natural inclination to avoid your emotional pain and instead examine it and understand it so that you can release it and therefore be more peaceful.

18. Do not allow your purpose in life to be driven by your subconscious thinking, make a conscious decision to make peace of mind your Purpose in life.

19. You will know you are making progress on the path to Living the Guided Life when things don't upset you as often, as intensely or not at all.

Chapter 20
CHECKING IN

At this point it is important to give you a specific method for "Checking In" with your Inner Guide. My experience of Checking In began with the coaching of my students.

You will remember that we described that people who hit bottom are often the ones who make the most dramatic shifts in their lives. It is because they came to an understanding that their judgments were not working. They realize that they "Don't Know" what is best for them. I would have this same experience in my work with my students. I would be coaching them through some type of upset and I would reach a point where I didn't know what to say or how to help my student.

My first experience of Checking In was with a young man who was struggling in his relationship with his father. We got to a point in our conversation where I did not know what to offer the student to help him with his situation. I leaned back in my chair and we both sat silently for a few moments. In my mind I had the following thoughts/ dialogue:

"Okay, there is supposedly this universal energy that can answer all questions. Then help resolve this situation because I don't know what to do."

At this point I began to talk with my student again. He left my office a few minutes later and I realized that after I had Checked In he and I were able to come up with some thoughts about the situation that left him feeling at peace. I was aware that everything shifted once I Checked In. The conversation quickly went from being stalled to being wrapping up quite easily and peacefully.

I was so struck by the sudden shift and the ease with which things resolved themselves that I realized this was no ordinary coaching session. My Checking In had a major impact on the tenor of the conversation.

This experience of a quick shift after Checking In had me excited. How far could I take this process? Luckily I work with students with very difficult lives who need coaching on a regular basis. Therefore I was able to repeat this experiment over and over again, and refine my technique.

When I am coaching my students, or an adult, there is almost always a point where I am not sure where to take the conversation next. In these moments I continued to acknowledge, "I Don't Know" and ask for guidance.

In that first experience of Checking In I spent some time afterwards reviewing exactly what happened so that I could work to repeat it, this process is described in chapter 5, "Success and Failures". This was clearly a success and I wanted to make sure I could repeat the process.

What did happen? I acknowledged that I did not know what to say, think or do (the "I Don't Know" mind), I asked for help and then I re-engaged in the conversation.

Let's break this process down. Step one, I acknowledged "I Don't Know". This is valuable because the I Don't Know mind (chapter 6) opens me up to Inner Guidance.

Step 2, I asked for help. Asking for help can be a block to Inner Guidance if you don't complete step 1. What I mean by this is if you ask for help and already have a preconceived idea of what the solution should be, you are not in the I Don't Know mind. You think you **know** what should happen.

This ties step 1 and step 2 together. Let's add step 3 and get the full picture of how to Check In. In the story of my first experience of consciously Checking In, the 3rd step was re-engaging in the conversation with my student. This is a highly significant part of the process that also ties into the first two steps.

Re-engaging in the conversation allowed my mind to let go of the idea that I had asked for help. This letting go is significant because it is telling my mind that my Inner Guide can handle the issue. This is not important to my Inner Guide. It loves me unconditionally and will always help. But, the more faith my mind has in my Inner Guide the more it will be open to its Guidance. By offering up the situation to my Inner Guide and then moving on with my life I am telling my mind (my ego mind) that I have faith in my Inner Guide.

A helpful analogy to this letting go process might be a co-worker. Let's say you have worked with someone for years and you know they are detailed and thorough in their work. When you pass off an assignment to them you don't worry, you know they will get the job done right. After passing off the assignment you can move on to other things without any hesitation or concern.

This letting go process also helps with getting my ego and my intellect out of the way. If I am searching for the answer or trying to figure something out my ego or my intellect will attempt to solve the problem. As we discussed in chapter 7, "Judgments Mine or Inner Guides", if you are being honest with yourself you will acknowledge that your ego and your intellect are very limited in their ability to help resolve difficulties.

One way to think about this is with our Inner Guide Radio (chapter 3) analogy. If I am choosing to tune into my intellect or my ego I can't tune into my Inner Guidance. My mind can only tune into one frequency at a time.

This re-engaging in the conversation is just one example of letting go. As you check in and ask for help you will move on with whatever you are doing in your day. Don't dwell on the problem or searching for the solution. Just as with that thorough co-worker, you know the job will get done and done right, let it go.

I was 40 when I had this first experience of consciously Checking In. In looking back at that experience I realize that in the years leading up to it I had done a tremendous amount of work on my subconscious pain (chapter 9). I had cleared enough pain and developed enough Peace of Mind that I was able to make that clear conscious connection with my Inner Guide.

This is why it is important that you work through the process described in this book. Specifically, chapter 16, "Beliefs, the Driving Force" and chapter 17, "Pain as the Gateway to Peace", offer a process for you to rid yourself of subconscious pain and develop greater peace of mind.

In several paragraphs in this chapter I have used the term, "Consciously" when I referred to Checking In. All of us have had moments in our lives when we were guided to make a decision that felt like the right choice. But, most people have these experiences periodically and are not able to easily repeat them. When I use the word consciously, I mean that you can make a choice in any moment to connect with your Inner Guidance.

One more thought about your Checking In process. When you are asking for help be as non-specific as possible. This sounds rather counterintuitive. I am telling you to ask for help with whatever the situation is but don't be very specific. Hold the issue in your mind and ask for help because you know something is bothering you.

By being non-specific you are again acknowledging that your Inner Guide is a better judge of the situation than you are. Not only do I not know the answer, I don't even understand all the complexities of the problem. Now you have really turned it over.

A nice frame of reference for this Checking In process is when you are engaged in an activity that completely occupies your mind. In the second chapter I refer to artists or athletes as experiencing being in the zone. If you have some activity that you engage in that completely engrosses you to the point where you are making intuitive decisions that work out beautifully this is a form of checking in. The process in this book will help you to live intuitively (connected to your Inner Guide) throughout your day.

Conclude with Gratitude

As you finish reading Living the Guided Life keep in mind that the material in this book is just a beginning. You will need to apply this material to your life on a daily basis not just store it away in your memory. Remember that making a foreign language your primary form of communication requires constant conscious effort at first. Eventually you will get to a place of naturally tuning into your Inner Guidance.

Lastly, be sure to express your gratitude for the Guidance that you receive. This is not for your Inner Guide, it is unconditionally loving so your gratitude will not impact it. But, it is valuable for you and your mind. You will be helping to reinforce in your mind that your Inner Guide is the most powerful form of help you can employ. It will also help you to recognize that the process worked. "Hey, I asked for help and received it. Thank you." You are much more likely to ask again when you have appreciated the outcome from previous queries.

Thank you, and may all your days be Guided!

Toolbox of ideas for Inner Guidance

1. Inner guidance trumps any other guidance.

2. Learning the language of Inner Guidance takes practice like learning a foreign language. Your Inner Guide is pure.

3. Your Inner Guide is **ALWAYS** broadcasting its message of peace, you need only to tune in.

4. Patience, less judgment and acceptance are mindsets that help you to match the frequency of your Inner Guide.

5. Pay attention to what thoughts bring you closer to Inner Guidance and repeat them as often as possible.

6. You must unlearn the language of judgment and learn the language of acceptance.

7. Your Inner Guide is the best judge of what is good for you!!

8. Acknowledging that you "Don't Know" what is best for you, opens you up to your Inner Guidance that does "Know" what is best for you.

9. You are tuned into the past because your thinking is mostly subconscious and the subconscious is filled with thoughts from the past.

10. People, things and events do not cause our feelings.

11. Your feelings are caused by **YOUR** thinking.

12. Being Inner Directed brings me closer to my Inner Guidance, being Outer Directed takes me farther from my Inner Guidance.

13. I must let go of my intellect's desire to be in control if I am to tune into my Inner Guide's broadcast.

14. You must let go of your belief that inflicting emotional punishment is the best way to help people change behaviors/evolve, this is not a frequency that your Inner Guide broadcasts on.

15. Taking personal responsibility for your feelings and choosing peaceful thoughts is a necessary first step in tuning into your Inner Guide.

16. Your subconscious false beliefs about yourself are driving your behavior.

17. Overcome your natural inclination to avoid your emotional pain and instead examine it and understand it so that you can release it and therefore be more peaceful.

18. Do not allow your purpose in life to be driven by your subconscious thinking, make a conscious decision to make peace of mind your Purpose in life.

19. You will know you are making progress on the path to Living the Guided Life when things don't upset you as often, as intensely or not at all.

20. Check In with your Inner Guide frequently, with an open mind. Acknowledge not knowing, ask for help and go about your day. Be grateful for the Guidance that you receive.

CLARIFICATION OF TERMS

Efficacy – The level of effectiveness with which someone is able to accomplish something.

Characteristics of Your Inner Guide – Pure, Unconditionally Loving, and Peaceful. Inner Guides only purpose is your peace of mind.

Emotions – Chemicals produced in your Hypothalamus, triggered by your thinking and released into your blood stream.

Experience – Your thoughts and subsequent feelings.

Inner Directed – A belief system that you are responsible for your experience (as defined above) of life, it is all happening inside of you.

Outer Directed – A belief system that the world outside of you is the cause of your experience of life.

"I Don't Know" mind – A state of mind whereby you decide that your intellect nor your ego knows what is best for you. This mindset opens you up to your Inner Guidance.

Sub- conscious mind – A process whereby your mind stores memories of the past and processes feelings of guilt and fear (simplified definition for the purposes of this book).

Conscious mind – Thoughts that you are aware of. A light, that when it is shone on the darkness of the subconscious mind dissipates the guilt and fear that is stored there.

Personal Responsibility – The recognition that you are able to choose your emotional response to everything and everyone.

The Driving Force – A belief or set of beliefs about yourself. These beliefs are maintained mostly in your subconscious mind and they drive your thinking and therefore your decisions and behavior.

Purpose – A consciously chosen defining or guiding principle that directs your thinking as well as your actions. This is distinguished from the Driving Force definition above because it is a ***conscious*** choice.

Checking In – The thought process of asking your Inner Guide for help.